Anthony Peake is a graduate of The University of Warwick and studied at postgraduate level at The London School of Economics and The University of Westminster. He is a member of the International Association of Near-Death Studies (IANDS), the International Association for the Study of Dreams (IASD), the Scientific & Medical Network and the Society For Psychical Research (PSR).

He runs a very active international web-based Forum in which his ideas and hypotheses are discussed and debated. This can be found at http://www.anthonypeake.com/forum

By the same Author

Is There Life After Death? – The Extraordinary Science of What Happens When You Die

The Daemon – A Guide To Your Extraordinary Secret Self

THE OUT-OF-BODY EXPERIENCE

The History and Science of Astral Travel

Anthony Peake

WATKINS PUBLISHING
LONDON

This edition first published in the UK and USA 2011 by
Watkins Publishing, Sixth Floor, Castle House,
75–76 Wells Street, London W1T 3QH

Text Copyright © Anthony Peake 2011

Anthony Peake has asserted his right under the Copyright, Designs
and Patents Act 1988 to be identified as the author of this work.

1 3 5 7 9 10 8 6 4 2

Designed and typeset by Jerry Goldie Graphic Design

Printed and bound in China by Imago

British Library Cataloguing-in-Publication Data Available

Library of Congress Cataloging-in-Publication Data Available

ISBN: 978-1-78028-021-9

www.watkinspublishing.co.uk

Distributed in the USA and Canada by Sterling Publishing Co., Inc.
387 Park Avenue South, New York, NY 10016-8810

For information about custom editions, special sales, premium and
corporate purchases, please contact Sterling Special Sales
Department at 800-805-5489 or specialsales@sterlingpub.com

Contents

Acknowledgements   vii
Foreword – by Ervin Laszlo   ix
Prologue   xiii

Part I – The Experience   1

1. Introduction   2
2. The Mystic Explanation   9
3. The Mystery of the Near-Death Experience   27
4. A Special Case: Robert Monroe   52
5. Remote Viewing: The Case of Ingo Swann   71
6. The Modern Groups   89
7. The Mystery of Lucid Dreaming   109

Part II – The Science   127

8. Neurology   128
9. The Psychedelic Route   138
10. The Physics   154
11. The 'Intrasomatic' Experience   191

Epilogue   209
Notes   213
Index   217

ACKNOWLEDGEMENTS

I would like to thank Dr Arthur Funkhouser and Tom Campbell for their advice and technical assistance regarding the quantum physics; the fantastic guys on my Forum; the Walker Group and last, but not least, my wife Penny for her continuing and unselfish support of me and my Daemon.

Foreword

Anthony Peake has written the most incredibly lucid and comprehensive book on the most incredibly complex and mysterious subject. It is a pleasure to write a few words to preface it and suggest that it should be read – read by everyone who has ever asked herself or himself whether what we perceive in the everyday world is *really* that world. And whether there are perceptions that are entirely beyond that world.

The answer to the first question is no, and to the second, yes. No, the world is most unlikely to be simply the way we perceive it, and yes, we also can perceive the world very differently from ordinary perceptions. (Bertrand Russell made short shrift of the first question. He said 'Common sense, if true, leads to physics. Physics, if true, shows that common sense is false. Therefore common sense, if true, is false. Therefore it's false.')

In light of modern science, physics in particular, the answer to the first question is reasonably unequivocal. But there is no clear answer to the more difficult question: what is the true nature of the world? And also, how is it that we can perceive the world so very differently? Not only from within our brain and body, but even from beyond... These are questions that have intrigued people through the ages, and they remain as important today as ever. They don't go away for being ignored, as modern people do when they adopt the facile and fashionable stance of down-to-earth scepticism.

Peake faces these difficult questions, for he has had experiences that he could not, and certainly did not wish to, ignore. He recounts in this book his own experiences, as well as a wide repertory of experiences by others, some anecdotal, others carefully tested. They are inexplicable in the context of down-to-earth pragmatism, yet they are insistently real. They are not even unusual, just frequently repressed and generally under-reported and under-investigated. It appears that our mind and brain can communicate with the world in strange and wonderful ways. And that the world itself is strange and wonderful in ways that nobody other than mystics and poets could envision.

Peake refers to my theories in tackling these questions, and I should add a few words on this score. Yes, I did say that the all-encompassing information- and memory-sea I call the 'Akashic Field' is rooted in the universe's zero-point field (ZPF). But in the last few years I modulated this simple, and perhaps all-too-simple, hypothesis. The ZPF is but one of the many physical manifestations of the deep structure of the universe. At the bottom of it all is very likely the field of fields that includes the ZPF with its zero-point energy, but includes far more than that. It also includes all universal and quantum fields, and the as yet little-understood holographic field that I believe conveys the non-local connection underlying micro- as well as macro-level entanglement. But all that I earlier claimed for the ZPF is valid for this super-grand-unified field. It is the in-itself unobservable matrix that grounds the observable universe. We cannot define it as a separate reality because every definition we could offer would be in terms of things – fields, forces, relations or entities – that are not only produced by this field, but are actually *in* this field. Or, more radically, *are* this field.

It is not as though there was the manifest world, *and* a fundamental field that grounds that world. World and field are one. This one-world is non-local; all of its elements are subtly but effectively linked. Microtubules, Bose-Einstein condensates, holograms, the implicate order, the ZPF, and the super-grand-unified Akashic Field are as many hypotheses for understanding its nature and its dynamics, and the possibilities for understanding it.

Peake offers a conscientious and comprehensive review of the relevant evidence for unusual and commonsensically inexplicable experiences, together with clear reasoning regarding the possible explanations. He brings us closer to understanding the mystery of the real world, and of the many ways that we can apprehend it. This is what this book is all about. It is about a great deal, as much or more than any book I have ever read. Reading it is a mind-expanding experience that must not be missed.

Ervin Laszlo

Prologue

Suddenly I was not too sure about this. What had seemed a good idea back home in England was looking less enticing as I watched her inventor coax Lucia into life. Lucia sat in the corner of the room almost insect-like, her single eye waiting to hold me in her gorgon-like gaze. Indeed I was reminded of the UFOs that wreaked destruction on mankind in the original 1950s' movie *War of the Worlds*.

I was at the home of writer Evelyn Elsaesser-Valarino on the shores of Lake Geneva in Switzerland. I had been invited over by Evelyn to meet Austrian psychologist Dr Engelbert Winkler and his associate, neurologist Dr Dirk Proeckl. Dr Winkler had read both my previous two books and was aware that I was part way through writing the book you are now reading. He was also aware that the subject matter of this book was the out-of-body experience and, as such, he was keen for me to experience, for myself, how such a state can be created at will.

The night before, over a wonderful meal in Geneva, Dr Winkler had explained to me in some detail how Lucia worked her magic. He told me that by combining stroboscopic light with differing brightness levels, he and Dr Proeckl had found a way whereby the brain wave patterns of a subject placed in front of the LL-stimulator can be changed to reflect the level normally seen in individuals who have spent years practising deep meditation techniques. However, because light was being used to stimulate reactions within the brain, Lucia sometimes also engendered transcendental experiences similar to those reported during near-death experiences and other altered states of consciousness.

Dr Winkler then described how, in April 2010, he and his associates had visited Tibet to evaluate the effectiveness of the LL-stimulator with one of the few groups in the world who could give a considered opinion – Buddhists trained in deep meditation techniques, particularly the form known as 'Dream Yoga'.

The results were astonishing. One monk stated that it was like 'seeing a mandala with one's eyes shut'. Another reported that the lamp made it possible for him to focus his spirit inward and cut out the outside world. He added that he felt that he had left his body behind and was in a state in which he was surrounded by vivid colours. Winkler and Proeckl were delighted that their neurological and psychological research was supported by such deeply meditative individuals.

For me, phenomena such as the out-of-body experience, lucid dreaming and other unusual psychological perceptions had been a lifelong interest, but I have never found myself experiencing anything that could be described as an altered state of consciousness.

And so it was that the next afternoon I gave myself up to the tender mercies of the 'lady' known as Lucia.

As Dr Winkler charged up the machine, I knew that the next 20 minutes could present me with strong subjective evidence for the existence of such states; otherwise they would forever be sensations described by others with which I could never really empathize.

I waited for my adventure to begin. I settled down in a reclining chair. Lucia was about three feet away with her set of lights positioned at my eye level. Dr Winkler told me to close my eyes. This I did and within seconds I heard the machine start up. I perceived through my closed eyelids a series of small flickering lights surrounding a larger central light that flashed on and off in a pre-programmed fashion. For two minutes or so I watched the flickering with mild interest. Then, quite unexpectedly, there was a series of explosions of blue light in the centre of my visual field. Seconds later, in my peripheral vision appeared a splash of yellow light that slowly spread across the image in front of me and, in doing so, it obscured the blue explosions. I was convinced that these lights were being caused by Dr Winkler changing the colours of the LL-stimulator. I asked if this was the case. I was told to open my eyes slightly. To my complete surprise the external light source was still pure white light with not a trace of colouration. These colours were being generated not by any external source but internally by my brain. I found this really quite odd.

But what happened next began to disturb me. My eyes started to vibrate in my head. It was a very unpleasant sensation. I told Dr Winkler about this. I then heard the voice of Dr Proeckl, the neurologist, who had clearly just entered the room. He told me not to worry and that what I was experiencing was a physiological, not neurological, reaction to the stroboscopic effects. After a few seconds, and much to my relief, the vibrating stopped and then I noticed something moving in my extreme right peripheral 'vision' field. I mentioned this and Dr Winkler told me to move my head round to look at what was there. He told me that my brain had now taken control of what I was experiencing and that the coloured lights would continue even if I turned my head to my right and, in doing so, moved my eyes away from the stimulator. I found this hard to believe but I did as instructed. I was amazed. The illumination continued even though I was no longer looking directly at Lucia. I turned my head and 'focused' on the disturbance. As it came into focus I felt my heart leap into my mouth. I knew that my body was still located in a room in a house near Geneva but part of me was somewhere else entirely.

I was looking down on a vast plain made up of a chessboard-like series of black and white squares. I could see the squares running off to a distant horizon that seemed to glow with a faint bluish light. I then realized that I was suspended many thousands of feet above the surface of the plain. My mind simply couldn't comprehend the sensation of dual location. However, my hands decided that this was a dangerous place to be and they grabbed the sides of the chair in a vice-like grip. The sensation of vertigo was palpable. Just as I was trying to come to terms with this the vibrations started again, but this time it was not only my eyes but my whole body. As the vibration levels increased I felt what seemed to be a massive rush of blood to my head and I felt myself rising out of the chair. Well, that is not quite true. I felt as if part of me was vibrating in and out of my body. I was convinced that the others in the room could see my body twitching up and down at a frighteningly rapid rate. I felt like an astronaut sitting at the top of an Apollo launch rocket as it accelerated into space. It was extremely scary but also stupendously amazing. Nevertheless, my fear overcame my fascination and I asked Dr Winkler to turn Lucia off. This he did and I was suddenly back in the reality I had felt so secure within for over 56 years.

Whatever had happened to me, and wherever I had journeyed to on that warm Swiss afternoon, it was not in what we term 'consensual space' – the place we share with others as part of our everyday experience of the world – this was another location altogether. I had experienced my first encounter with the subject of my planned book, an encounter that was to change totally my approach to this intriguing subject.

My experience made me realize that I had been asking the wrong questions. To try to discover if the out-of-body experience is real or imagined is to miss the point entirely. What I should have been doing was enquiring into the very nature of perception itself and, by implication, the nature of the phenomenal world that our senses tell us is so real.

The book you now have in your hands is a record of my personal quest to understand what happened to me that day in Switzerland and to incorporate that experience into the model I was already in the process of developing. In its pages I will review the evidence that such altered states of consciousness are subjectively real experiences; I will delve into the science by which consciousness can seemingly locate itself outside of the body and I will, finally, present my own hypotheses as to what may be happening when a person experiences such perceptions. As with all my books, I will simply present the information. It is you, dear reader, who will finally decide whether you accept my conclusions or not.

Part I

The
Experience

CHAPTER 1

Introduction

The Malaya Experience

Over the last few years my life has become a very strange one. Although I have been interested in what many people term 'weird phenomena' since my early teens it is only since the publication of my first book, *Is There Life After Death? – The Extraordinary Science of What Happens When We Die* that I have met with many, many people who have experienced such things first-hand.

I, on the other hand, have only experienced a handful of odd events in my life and these simply pale into insignificance when compared with the amazing events that are explained to me when I do my lectures, emailed to me by readers of my books or now posted on my internet Forum. But the strangest thing is that for the most part I am regularly struck by just how down-to-earth and 'normal' these experiencers are. They are ordinary people who have had extraordinary events take place for which they have no explanation. Indeed, many confide in me because they are scared that by telling their friends and associates of their experiences they will be branded as needing psychiatric treatment.

After the publication of my second book *The Daemon – A Guide to your Extraordinary Secret Self* interest in me and my ideas increased to the extent that I suddenly found myself being invited regularly onto radio programmes in the United Kingdom and the United States. With my profile raised, more and more people contacted me. I was forced to conclude that extraordinary events were not rare at all. Indeed they were phenomenally common. It was clear to me that these people were keen to have their story told because they wanted *answers*, proper answers that could *explain* exactly what took place when they experienced the inexplicable.

Then one Monday I was doing my regular afternoon slot on BBC Merseyside. Each fortnight I pick a topic and discuss it with Billy Butler, a popular local celebrity who is known for his down-to-earth approach and sharp sense of humour. Billy is the ideal host and he always manages to ask the questions of me that the average listener would want to ask. This particular afternoon my chosen subject was the out-of-body experience. It was a subject with which I had only passing acquaintance. However, I knew enough to give a quick review of what the OBE, as it is generally known, was about. I explained that occasionally, and usually under times of stress or fear, people claim to find themselves outside of their body and viewing the world around them from another location. Others claim that they can visit distant locations in this state; and that they even encounter other beings, some human, some not.

As I was describing this I could tell that Billy was finding it all a little too weird for his taste. He asked me how this could be; what scientific evidence there was for such a circumstance. I answered that I didn't know enough about the subject, but it was something that I was keen to pursue. Steve Coleman, Billy's producer, then messaged us through our headphones saying that there was a caller keen to get through and speak to us 'on air'. Billy and I agreed and after a few seconds the caller was in contact with us.

The caller was keen to discuss with us an event that had taken place many years before when he was doing his army national service in Malaya (now Malaysia) in the late 1950s. He explained that he had been up all night on watch duties and had just returned to the barracks. As he sat on his bunk he realized that he had forgotten to wake the next soldier who was due to replace him outside. He got up and began to walk across the room to his fellow soldier's bunk. As he did so he felt rather strange. His body felt odd. For some reason he turned round and looked back at his bunk. To his absolute shock he saw himself still sitting on the bed staring into space. Quite naturally this scared the hell out of him and he rushed back across the room to jump back into his body. The next thing he knew he was waking up in his bunk a few hours later.

It was clear from his tone of voice that this event had long been a mystery to him. He simply could not understand how he could find himself out of his body, looking at himself from a short distance away. He was seeking an explanation because he was not dying at the time, he was simply exhausted, but something strange had happened that sultry night many years ago; something that to him was completely inexplicable.

I tried my normal approach of playing the devil's advocate. Could he have been asleep at the time, I asked. 'No' came the very precise reply: 'I was tired but I was wide awake.' This man was absolutely adamant that for a few seconds, over 50 years ago, he experienced something that is totally inexplicable within our modern scientific understanding of how the world works. People cannot simply leave their body and go wandering round in the external world. Consciousness is created by the brain and is located within the brain. To suggest that consciousness can exist outside of the brain means that our whole materialistic model is wrong – that a person's mind can exist without the need of a body to supply it with oxygen, eyes to process light waves and ears to process sound waves. Furthermore, it means that consciousness can move itself around in the external world without any obvious way of doing so. In his disembodied state the young soldier had no legs to move him across the barrack floor. How could he have 'walked' anywhere?

When the caller finished describing his experience it was clear that both Billy and I were quite stunned. Here again was a seemingly normal, well-balanced elderly gentleman who was describing the most extraordinary event on live radio.

Suzanne Segal

On returning home my interest in the out-of-body experience had really been stimulated. I began to read up about the subject and again, to my surprise, found that it was a much commoner phenomenon than I had assumed. Indeed, I further discovered that modern psychologists and psychiatrists are not at all dismissive of this phenomenon and many interesting studies have taken place in recent years. Furthermore, scientists have sensibly replaced the rather cumbersome and negatively coloured out-of-body-experience term for something less likely to raise negative reactions. The new term is 'ecsomatic'. This is a far more precise word that covers all experiences in which consciousness seems to be outside of the body. Indeed that is exactly what ecsomatic means – 'ec' indicating outside and 'soma' is a Latin term for body.

I was surprised to find that many academic papers had been written on the subject and that hundreds of cases had been recorded. One in particular caught my attention. It involved a young American woman called Suzanne Segal who was living in Paris in the early 1980s.

In the spring of 1982 she was waiting for a bus to take her home from a birthing class when something very strange took place. As the bus approached she felt her ears pop and suddenly she felt as if she was enclosed in some kind of force field that was surrounding her and making itself a barrier between her and the external world. For a few seconds she was totally disorientated and then she found that her body was acting as if it was not really under her control. What happened next was to change her life. In her book *Collision with the Infinite* she describes the incident:

> I lifted my right foot to step up into the bus and collided head-on with an invisible force that entered my awareness like a silently exploding stick of dynamite, blowing the door of my usual consciousness open and off its hinges, splitting me in two. In the gaping space that appeared, what I had previously called 'me' was forcefully pushed out of its usual location inside me into a new location that was approximately a foot behind and to the left of my head. 'I' was now behind my body looking out at the world without using the body's eyes.[1]

She was suddenly outside of her body, existing in a space behind and to the left of her corporeal being. She described her new location in time and space as a 'cloud of awareness'.

This was a similar, but even more powerful, version of what happened to my caller on BBC Merseyside. This experience totally changed Segal's life and from then onwards she seemed to exist in two worlds. But what was happening to her, and all the other experiencers? Are they all simply delusional or, even worse, simply liars seeking attention? Well I cannot really speak for Suzanne Segal as I have never met her. However, on reading her book I am of the opinion that she was a very well balanced, ordinary young woman. Indeed, I would have attempted to contact her to discuss the events with her but, tragically, and possibly significantly, she died in 1997 of a brain tumour.

It is important to acknowledge that science may be at the start of a new paradigm that can accommodate such anomalies as the one described to me that afternoon in the radio studio. Indeed, many open-minded scientists regularly observe that the next catalyst will be a breakthrough in our understanding of the nature of consciousness. This is because consciousness, and its implications, present insurmountable problems with regard to the present scientific paradigm. Self-awareness within a seemingly unaware universe simply does not make sense, and psychic phenomena similarly present anomalies that may be the pointers to a hitherto unknown model of science; a model in which mind creates matter rather than matter creates mind.

But there are many other 'anomalies' that fail to fit into the present paradigm. As one example, scientists readily admit that 71.3 per cent of our universe is missing.[2] This 71.3 per cent consists of something called 'dark energy'. It is called this because nobody has a clue what it really is. They just know that in order for the universe to be balanced this stuff has to exist. What is even weirder is that the remaining 28.7 per cent is made up of what is known as 'baryonic matter' and another mysterious substance known as 'dark matter'. Baryonic matter is everything that we observe in the physical universe; in fact this is 'matter' as we know it to be and is defined as having location, extension and mass. Dark matter is another unknown form of matter that we know exists because its gravitational pull affects baryonic matter. So the physical universe that our modern paradigm puts much store upon is only a tiny part of a greater universe that we simply cannot detect.

Could it be that the explanation to what happened to my phone contact and to Suzanne Segal can be found within the mysteries of 'dark energy' and consciousness?

The book you now have in your hands is the result of ten months of intense reading and networking. I have managed to discuss the ecsomatic experience with some of the most important practitioners and experiencers in the world. I have also reviewed much of the latest material from the world of science, from neurology to quantum physics. In doing so I genuinely believe that I have come up with a hypothesis that may, just may, help to explain what is happening. If I am right it means that what we understand to be reality is not at all what we believe it to be.

In the remaining pages I will present the history, review the evidence, and then present the model. In keeping with modern scientific terminology and in order to avoid confusion I will refer to the out-of-body experience and the 'ecsomatic experience' as interchangeable terms depending upon context.

As always with my books, it is you, the reader, who will decide if what I present makes rational or logical sense. And, as before, the debate and discussion will be open to all on my international Forum at www.anthonypeake.com/forum.

CHAPTER 2

The Mystic Explanation

Defining The Territory

Over the last five years I have met with many individuals who have patiently explained to me that the model of the universe I present in my previous books is reflected in the mystic tradition that has been carried through by adepts and teachers from the most ancient of times. However, we have never really discussed in any detail the idea that consciousness could leave its bodily shell and travel to other locations both within the external world that we all seem to share, and to much more exotic places that are just as real.

I have met and become friends with individuals who had been trained in shamanistic, kabbalistic, theosophist and modern mystical traditions, but we always avoided this area of debate. This may have been because my books suggest a fairly materialist model of the mind. I propose a model whereby it is within the realms of the mind itself that magical places can be encountered. The external world, for most people, is a brain-generated illusion similar to the world as presented in the movies *The Matrix* and *Vanilla Sky*. As such, the idea that the person could project their mind into external space and travel within it did not really fit.

However, when I explained that my next book was to be a review of the ecsomatic experience, my associates started to tentatively explain that maybe my model, now known as the Bohmian IMAX, may not be the full, or even partial, explanation for many mysterious altered states of consciousness. They suggested to me that the worlds visited during ecsomatic states are very real and had been long known to be real. Indeed, they added that I may be surprised to discover that most of the great religious traditions had models of reality that involved ecsomatic travelling.

And so it was that my journey began by listening carefully to what I was told about these traditions. This chapter will present a review of the things I found and, how, at the end of my historical review, I was surprised to discover that my model and the model of esoteric mysticism were suddenly not that far apart. It was simply a question of perspective.

The Territory of Transcendence

For many people there is only one world – the physical world. We can travel in this world by using our bodies to move around. This world is consistent in that when we close our eyes it is unchanged when we open them. Let us call this the 'consensual world'. The consensual world is shared with other human beings, animals and inanimate objects, all of which seem to exist in a three-dimensional space. When we go to sleep and then wake up, the consensual world may have evolved during our period of absence, but for the most part it remains the same. The people we knew before we went to sleep are virtually unchanged and it is the same for their person-alities and motivations.

However, when we leave the consensual world and enter the dream world everything changes. The consensual world seems to recede from us and we enter another place that is not consistent. This world does not have continuity or a definitive map or geography. The laws of science do not seem to apply in this place and people we encounter in this world are not consistent. Indeed we may encounter people who we know to be dead. We may find that we can fly. We may meet mythical creatures and encounter strange places and locations. Time similarly seems to become elastic and malleable. When we eventually awake we are back in the consensual world, which remains consistent and trustworthy. The next time we sleep we are catapulted back into the dream world, but usually a very different one from the one we left. The dream world is defined by its lack of continuity or permanence.

As far back as written records can take us, and it is fairly reasonable to conclude, as far back as man has discussed his inner world with his fellow human beings, this place of dreams and hallucinations has presented a window to another reality. This is the place where man can encounter the spirit world, and possibly the domain of the gods. Throughout the millennia, mystics, magicians and saints have encountered this alternative world and experienced it on their own terms, and in doing so have devised techniques and processes whereby this place can be entered and left at will. These 'travellers' have reported back to their associates a geography and a structure of these 'Astral Planes' that are surprisingly consistent. It is to these mystic traditions that we will now turn our attention.

Shamanism

Shamanism is recognized as being the world's oldest religion. Records of its rituals have been found in cave paintings dating back as far as 6000BC.

The word 'saman' is derived from the language of the Tungus people of Siberia. This was transliterated into Russian as 'shaman'. This has been interpreted to mean 'he who knows,' or 'one who is excited, moved, raised'. In general it has been applied to many traditional figures including medicine men, necromancers and ecstatics, but essentially the shaman is an indigenous practitioner whose expertise lies in entering a trance that enables his or her soul to travel to the upper and lower worlds of the spirits and demons. The shaman 'journeys' through this altered state of consciousness in order to pass into the world of the spirits as a mediator for his tribe or people.

Becoming a shaman may involve an inheritance, in that the ability to travel into the upper and lower worlds has been handed down within families, but usually the individual is seen to have odd traits that suggest shamanic abilities. These may include spontaneous trance states, ecstatic or deranged behaviour or even possession.

Siberia is considered the homeland of the shaman but the tradition slowly spread across northern Asia into North, Central and South America. It is reasonable to conclude that the belief-system followed the migration routes of the North Asian people across the ancient land bridge between Siberia and Alaska and then down through continental America.

Although the ritual and traditions have changed over the millennia, shamanism still has a series of core beliefs; the one relevant to us is the belief in the ability of a shaman to leave the body and visit other planes of existence.

I am in the fortunate position of knowing a handful of individuals trained in the shamanic tradition. These include Gary Plunkett and Sebastian Cheatham, both of whom regularly experience shamanic journeys and train others in how to achieve these altered states of consciousness.

Gary informed me that to successfully negotiate the upper and lower levels of the shamanic universe the traveller must be trained to understand the symbols and the archetypes that will be encountered on entering these disincarnate realms.

In order to raise consciousness sufficiently to reach a state whereby the shamanic journey can begin, the brain has to be taken out of its normal state. A popular method of doing this is shamanic drumming. Any repetitive beat will do this, as aficionados of modern 'rave culture' will attest, but the power and rhythm of drumbeats seem particularly effective. As the mind concentrates upon the drums it goes into a trance state. The shamanic traveller then transfers to another place. This is called 'middle world' and may seem identical to our normal world but it is not. The traveller may feel that nothing has happened. However, Gary explained to me that the best way to test this is to jump up and down. In middle world the traveller may find that they continue to rise up in the air without coming back down to Earth.

Is this not identical to a classic ecsomatic experience? The floating sensation is one of the first things that an ecsomatic experiencer feels when in an out-of-body state – floating near the ceiling or at a point a certain distance behind and above the body. It is important to note that for those trained in the shamanic tradition this place is not consensual reality but another realm that is identical in every way.

Gary explained to me that middle world, although real, is created from the brain's memory banks and will contain archetypes and symbols personal to the traveller. In other words it is created from the memories of the experiencer. As such, the seemingly external environment of middle world is modelled by the mind from information it already has. It is like the fact that I have an image in my mind of what is behind my head at the moment. I know in general terms what should be there because I have sat at this desk in my study many times. I can visualize a fairly accurate model, and I am sure that in a semi-dream state I could create an image in my visual field.

Once a shamanic traveller realizes that they are in middle world they then need to search out their shamanic guide, or totem. This is always an animal and it will approach the traveller soon after reaching middle world. Sometimes, another being will be encountered. This is usually in humanoid form and is called 'the teacher'. The teacher will manifest in the image of an archetype specific to the traveller. This may be a character from fiction or film. For example, in recent years many travellers encounter Gandalf from the *The Lord of the Rings*, Spock from *Star Trek* or Obi Wan Kenobi from the *Star Wars* movies. These are all wisdom archetypes and, being characters from fiction, they are obviously internally generated archetypes.

The totem or the teacher will help the traveller find something called 'the portal'. In different traditions this can vary, but usually it will be a gate, door or other form of entrance. In the Celtic tradition it is usually a tree with an anomalous doorway or entrance in its trunk. This reminds me of the imagery in Guillermo del Toro's wonderful movie *Pan's Labyrinth* in which the young heroine, Ofelia, begins her journey to the underworld though a hole in an old tree. Clearly del Toro is using the imagery of European shamanic traditions to develop his powerful, and extremely moving, story.

Once the portal is found the shamanic traveller enters through it and will discover a facility to go up or down. With the help of the totem they will decide which way to go. If they go up they will enter what is, not surprisingly, called the 'upper world' and if they go down they find themselves in the 'lower world'.

If a traveller on their shamanic journey decides to go to the upper world, here they will find a place that is ethereal and full of clouds and mist. Indeed, travellers may find themselves flying within the clouds before landing somewhere and encountering many beings, some human, some animal, all of which are there to assist a shaman in developing their shamanic skills.

Within the shamanic tradition the lower world is a place with no boundaries but with a strong feeling of natural beauty. It is a very natural environment of jungle, desert or arctic conditions.

I was intrigued by the implications of the shamanic model because it clearly suggested that the ecsomatic experience involved a quest that included an inner journey within the furthest reaches of the mind, as much as a series of encounters in a real place that existed in the consensual world. Indeed, in my discussions with my shaman contacts, it became clear that what is encountered is a series of worlds full of archetypes pulled up from the deepest areas of the subconscious mind. However, what is of significance is that these beings seem to have motivations of their own, as if they have an existence independent of the shamanic traveller. This implied to me that although these worlds may be a creation of the mind, they also have a reality that challenges our present materialistic model of how the universe functions.

Shamanism cannot really be termed a religion in the general sense of the religions that were to follow it. It has no written tradition and no real rituals. However, its belief in levels of existence beyond the physical world became incorporated into many of the more organized belief systems of the Asiatic land mass, none more so than the religions of northern India, Tibet and Nepal.

Religions of Southeast Asia

The Indian subcontinent has been inhabited for millennia and has evidence of some of the oldest civilizations on the planet. Therefore, it is not at all surprising that sophisticated and complex religious beliefs developed in this area.

The earliest, and probably most influential, is a series of beliefs that are collectively known as Hinduism. It is believed that this religion-cum-philosophy is probably the most ancient living world religion, being at least 5,000 years old. Although generally associated with the Indian subcontinent, it has spread across Asia and now has adherents across the globe. In many ways it is a way of life rather than just a religion.

It is a commonly held belief that Hindus worship many gods. This is a misunderstanding of the basic tenet of Hinduism, that of the role of Brahman. Brahman is the Absolute – meaning, a being that is without form, who pervades everything, is present everywhere, is all-knowing, all-powerful and transcends space and time. In simple terms everything that is, is Brahman, and that includes every living creature, including man.

The material universe that we perceive with our senses is *maya*, an illusion, a dream world of Brahman. We, as such, being elements of Brahman, exist within a lucid dream that we collectively (as Brahman) are dreaming. What we consider to be our physical body is made up of an element that exists within *maya* and a subtle body, known as the *Sukshma sarira* or *Sukshma sharira*. The physical body is simply a container for the subtle body and at death the *Sukshma* simply reincarnates into a new life. Contained within this subtle body is the *Liṅga Śarīra*. This is the equivalent of what we know as conscious awareness.

Within the ancient writings of Hinduism can be found many

references to the idea that the subtle body and the *Liṅga Śarīra* can leave the confines of the physical body and journey to other places. For example, in these writings can be found references to what are known as the eight *siddhis*. These are supernormal powers that can be developed by deep meditation and study. The sixth *siddhi* is described as 'flying in the air'. Many commentators consider this to mean out-of-the-body experiences.

Of course in a belief system proposing that the physical world is simply the dream of Brahman, it is axiomatic to assume the subtle body can travel wherever it wishes within this dreamscape, the only restriction being lack of imagination.

In 566BCE a prince by the name of Gautama Siddhartha was born in the country now known as Nepal. His father was the king of the Hindu Sakya people and the young Gautama was brought up within the Hindu belief system. However, at the age of 30 he left home in search of enlightenment and five years later he found it sitting under a Bodhi tree in a place called Bodh Gaya in present-day Bihar. As soon as he came out of his meditative state he was a buddha, an enlightened being. From this day on he wandered the countryside preaching his new vision of how man should live his life. By the time of his death in Kusingara in Oudh, his new religion had peacefully grown out of Hinduism and within a handful of decades had spread across the whole of Southern Asia.

Although Buddhism took root across most of Southern and Southeast Asia, it is in the mountains of Tibet that it developed a strong mystical element; where, scholars believe, it encountered and assimilated many concepts from a much older, shamanistic tradition. Indeed, one school of Tibetan Buddhism still applies these beliefs as part of its teachings. Known as Bön, this school venerates a small structure in the brain known as the pineal gland. For the followers of Bön this organ is a gateway to alternate states of consciousness.

Another, later, Tibetan school that is of particular interest with regard to ecsomatic experiences is Vajrayana Buddhism. According to the teachings of this school there is a process called 'Dream Yoga'. The Tibetans believe that there are three states of mind. These are waking life, sleep and dreaming. They consider that these states correspond to life, death and rebirth.

Possibly of great significance to our quest for an understanding of the ecsomatic experience, it was members of the Bön and 'Dream Yoga' traditions who tested out the LL-stimulator when Dr Winkler and his associates travelled to Tibet in April 2010. It will be recalled from the prologue that the practitioners of this ancient, quasi-shamanistic tradition considered that the effect of the light stimulator was profound. In this tradition the non-dual source of consciousness is described as a multicoloured sphere of light – exactly what was described by the Tibetans when they experienced the stimulator. A few days later Dr Winkler, on a visit to the Potala Palace in Lhasa, noticed a much-revered selection of ossified elephant pineal glands. On asking questions he was informed that these were extremely holy relics for the followers of the Bön tradition. We shall discover later just how significant this may prove to be in regard to a possible explanation for the ecsomatic experience.

It is important to try to become lucid in dreams during life, because to do so helps the person appreciate what is really taking place when encountering the dreaded 'bardo' state in the afterlife. If you have become lucid you will know that the bardo state is a creation of the mind. If not, you will assume that it is real and simply an extension of waking life. What helps in understanding this is a concept known as the 'clear light of death'. In effect this clear light is the person's 'true self' and in merging with this light the soul can avoid the compulsory rebirth that is forced upon those who remain in the bardo state, ignorant of its true purpose. In becoming literally an 'enlightened being' the soul remembers all its previous lives and can decide if it wishes to return to follow the cycle of birth and death again.

The Buddhist texts of the Tantra school teach how it is possible to gain lucidity in the dream state by encountering the 'clear light of sleep'. As it suggests this is a related state to the 'clear light of death' that can be encountered in borderlands between waking life and sleep. If this is done successfully then the person becomes lucid within the dream state.

In the Dzogchen teachings the ultimate goal is to be lucid during waking life as well as the dream state. This is an important point. According to the esoteric schools of Buddhism all human beings are in a state of permanent unenlightenment. They believe that they are fully aware during waking life, but this is another illusion. Only by carrying the clear light into the waking life can a person really become aware that what we perceive in the waking life is, in fact, a projection of the mind. On reaching this understanding the person can be liberated from the mind-forged manacles and become a literal 'Rainbow Being', a being made of light itself. On death all that will remain of the corpse will be fingernails and hair.

Such concepts have long been part of the traditions of the great religions of Asia whose central belief system states that the world is simply a mind-created illusion. However, it may come as some surprise to those unaware of such things, but the great Western religions all have at their core esoteric traditions suggesting that physical matter is not what it seems and that there are worlds behind the world presented to us by our senses.

The major tradition, and one that probably influenced similar beliefs within Christianity (Gnosticism) and Islam (Sufism), is the Jewish mystery school known as Kabbalah.

Kabbalah

For the Kabbalists everything that *is* emanates from what is known as 'The One'. By this they mean YHVH. This being is beyond all understanding. Indeed, 'he' can only be defined by what he is not. The One is a unity of all things. As such, nothing can be written about YHVA other than he is. Within this teaching YHVA is 'nothingness', because he is literally outside of human cognition.

For some unknown, and unknowable, reason 'The One' set in motion the process that ultimately led to the visible world that we perceive. However, our world is the last of a series of 'emanations' that spread out from YHVA, each one slightly more physical than the one from which it emanated. Initially there is the purity of spirit, and as we move through the various emanations we reach a point whereby 'spirit' becomes enclosed in matter.

The highest world is known as Atziluth. This is closest to the 'Limitless Light' that is the Divine Mind. This is also known as the world of Fire. The next is known as Beriah – the world in which the 'archetypes' can be found. Like Plato's 'Forms' these are the purest realities of the universals apprehended by the mind. In reflection of the four elements this is the world of Air. In this cosmology it acts as a barrier between Atziluth and the next level, one of great importance for any ecsomatic experience. This is called Yetzirah and is the equivalent of the astral plane. This is known as the world of Water. Finally we have the material world that the physical body exists within. This is known as Assiah (Action).

In Kabbalistic tradition every human psyche consists of three related elements. The element closest to the Divine is known as the *Yechidah*. In turn, this being has three elements; the Divine Self (*Yechidah*), True Will (*Chiah*) and Intuition (*Neshamah*). The everyday self, the being that calls itself 'I' and exists within the material world, is called the *Ruach*. The Ruach is linked with earth and the Yechidah with fire. This is a reflection of their true natures. The Ruach is rooted within the world of physical matter whereas the Yechidah is far more ethereal, reflecting the way in which fire seems to behave. For example, fire always rises above the earth and seems to flit in and out of existence.

The physical body, known as *Guph*, is an extension of the lower self. This is unthinking and has no spiritual aspects. It is rooted in the physical world and on death returns to its physical constituents.

The Ruach exists within Assiah. This is the everyday world of matter, rooted in the physical and following all the physical laws that have been discovered by materialistic science. However, in dreams and altered states, the world of Yetzirah can be encountered, if only for a short while. Whilst in these states the Ruach can perceive astonishing insights and intuitions. This model is closely in keeping with the experiences of the ecsomatic travellers that we will encounter in this book. Indeed, this model will be swiftly recognized in relation to the experiences of such projectors as Robert Monroe and Ingo Swann.

According to the teachings of the Kabbalah, the universe consists of 10 levels, spheres or sephiroth. These are Hokmah, Kether, Yesod, Hod, Netzach, Tiphareth, Geburah, Chesed, Binah and Malkuth. In September 1994 the founder and president of the Philosophers of Nature, Jean Dubuis, lectured on the true nature of reality from a modern Kabbalistic viewpoint. It is important to be aware that Dubuis is a trained scientist, working as a nuclear physicist with Nobel Prize winner Jolliot Curie. He acknowledged that during an out-of-body experience, or during a lucid dream, the traveller will reach one of the seven available sephiroth. According to Dubuis these are the clues to identification of location:

Yesod: A place of pale light often charged with the thought-forms of Earth.

Hod: A fairy-tale palace, complete with a magical oratory, alchemical lab and an astrological observatory. For some reason Hod can be frightening.

Netzach: Inspired by nature, green things predominate there. It may appear as a half-tree, or as a luxuriously coloured palace, or as a combination of both.

Tiphareth: Like the palace of the French kings, at Versailles, complete with fleur-de-lis. It is bright, with large windows, and the sky is always blue.

Geburah: A citadel, but comfortable.

Chesed: Often an enormous religious building, or a castle with a large temple enclosed in it.

Binah: Often experienced as a pyramid or a massive temple with a single spire.

Hokmah and Kether are beyond comprehension and therefore cannot be perceived during an OBE. He describes these as:

> Hokmah and Kether exist beyond the imagery of the psyche. At best one could say Hokmah would be an experience of spacelessness – or everything in creation existing in the same place – and Kether as a single point. Clearly, these two are closely related and are really aspects of the same thing: unity that exists at all levels.

Finally he mentions the earthly plane:

Malkuth: Our physical world with all the Earth being
             its temple.[3]

What is interesting in this is that Dubuis implies that we do not travel astrally within our own sephiroth. This rather contradicts the reports of OBEs related to a near-death state, and spontaneous or self-induced OBEs as described by many who experience these states. If Dubuis is right, it would explain why all attempts to gain proof of OBEs have been disappointing in the extreme and that in effect what are reported as OBEs are, in fact, lucid dreams or visits to other sephiroth that may seem 'Malkuth'-like.

The teachings of Kabbalah have had a profound influence on many Western mystical schools. The general model as described above is mirrored in the Hermetic traditions of the Renaissance and carried through to many secret and semi-secret esoteric schools, such as The Order of the Golden Dawn, The Builders of the Adytum, The Society of the Inner Light and the largest and most influential of the modern groups, The Servants of the Light. However, the major group to present these concepts to the public at large is the Theosophists and it is to their teachings that we now turn our attention.

Theosophy

In the late 19th century there was a great spiritual revival in the Western world. As well as an increased fervour within Christianity, there was also a new interest in the teachings of the religions of the Near East and South Asia, specifically the Jewish Kabbalah and the esoteric teachings of Hinduism and Buddhism.

Of all these groups the one that had the most influence was Theosophy, and still thrives today with lodges found across the

English-speaking world. Indeed, much of the teaching of Theosophy has close similarities to 'Dream Yoga' and the teachings of the Dzogchen School discussed earlier. It is reasonable to conclude that the founder of this movement, Helena Blavatsky, learned of such concepts during her travels in Tibet in the 1850s.

Theosophy teaches that there are many imperceptible levels of mind and reality and these can be travelled through, both internally and externally. These levels are populated with many sentient beings; some of them are hostile and others wish to assist in the evolution of humanity, both collectively and individually.

We are trapped in the illusion of matter. This is the lowest plane of existence. As one moves up through the planes, the density decreases until, in the highest plane, the seventh, all that exists is pure spirit. Human beings, according to Blavatsky, are evolving through these planes with the ultimate aim of becoming purely spiritual beings.

What is of interest is that Theosophy teaches that these levels overlap so, in effect, there is a part of the second plane that is accessible to a person within the first plane. Blavatsky suggests that other planes can be experienced but only by particularly advanced human beings who have spent many lifetimes training themselves to do so.

These advanced individuals are adepts and are known for their extreme spirituality within this plane. They usually become spiritual teachers, such as the Buddha and Jesus.

Just as there are Seven Planes so we all have seven bodies, each one reflecting the ever-decreasing density of the corresponding plane.

The physical body is termed 'the etheric'. This body coincides with the soma but it is not fully matter. Within its structure are several centres of awareness and energy. These are called 'chakras'. In keeping with the overall theme there are seven main chakras and they act as conductors for the 'kundalini' or 'earth energy'. However, it is the next body that is of significance for ecsomatic experiences. This is the 'astral body', which has the same material consistency as the astral plane and can travel within this plane during sleep states.

However, and this is of some significance, the Theosophists believe that the etheric body can travel to other locations within the earth plane if it can access the region that overlaps between this and the astral plane. Could this be the equivalent of the classic out-of-body experience as reported? According to Blavatsky, her Tibetan teachers had informed her that the most important organ of the body is the pineal gland. She wrote:

> (The pineal gland) is in truth the very seat of the highest and divinest consciousness in man, his omniscient, spiritual and all-embracing mind.[4]

This theme was picked up by her student CW Leadbeater who proposed that the pineal gland was the focus of energies received from the higher planes. Indeed, Leadbeater further proposed that the concept of a 'soul' was incorrect: man evolves through the seven bodies and gradually becomes spiritual in stages.

It is obvious that Blavatsky was not the originator of this proposal, but she was one of the first to publish secret information that she claimed had been handed down throughout the centuries. We shall discover just how intriguing this observation is when we review the neurological causes of the ecsomatic experience in a later chapter.

Blavatsky and the Theosophists also introduced another concept to Western thought that is now causing great interest within the fields of cosmology and quantum physics, something they termed the 'Akashic Record'. The term *akasha* is a Sanskrit expression that means 'sky' or 'aether'. This mystical substance is everywhere and within it is recorded every action, emotion, thought, feeling and experience of every living being. It is like a huge database that contains a record of everything. Mystics have long suggested that this information can be accessed in certain states of raised consciousness and the data can be downloaded for future use.

Blavatsky described the *akasha* as the universal life-force that manifests itself within living beings as something that had been known to occultists through the centuries as the *anima mundi*, the 'soul of the world'. The Akashic Record or 'Book of Life' is the Theosophist term for the information stored within the *akasha*.

As we shall discover later, when we encounter the science of ecsomatic experiences, this concept is far more than a mere mystical ideal, it may well be a crucial element in our understanding of what is really taking place when someone perceives that they leave their body and travel to other locations.

Conclusion

Of course all the above examples of traditional and mystical beliefs are based upon subjective experiences. These observations may have been based upon 'real' experiences, but the reality only goes as far as the inner experience of the mystic, shaman or adept. Although fascinating to discuss, such material contains no 'evidence' that can be considered 'scientific'. However, another mystery that has been reported for centuries is a phenomenon we now know as the near-death experience. In recent years there has been a massive interest in this subject and many best-selling books have been written describing what has been reported to take place when human consciousness approaches death. There are many differing descriptions but there is one constant that all experiencers describe: the sensation of leaving the body and travelling to another place in which self-awareness continues. It is to this fascinating phenomenon that we now turn our attention.

CHAPTER 3

The Mystery of the Near-Death Experience

George Ritchie & Raymond Moody

I have been a professional member of an organization called The International Association of Near Death Studies (IANDS) for nearly 10 years. What attracted to me to this association of medical professionals, psychiatrists, psychologists and enthusiastic lay people was their interest in the phenomenon known as the near-death experience or NDE. I had long been fascinated by the implications of this curious psychological state that has been reported since records began. For me the NDE, if understood in more detail, was a possible way in which so-called psychic phenomena may be explained using scientific methods. After many years of reading voluminous amounts about the NDE I am still of this opinion. Furthermore, I believe that the out-of-body aspects of the NDE are of crucial importance in helping us understand the mechanisms of both phenomena. It is my intention to review the close relationship between near-death and, in some cases actual death, experiences and the out-of-body experience. I will also attempt to present some counter-explanations, which suggest that the phenomenon may simply be a hallucination created by the dying brain.

The modern interest in the subject began in the mid 1960s when a young philosophy student came across a very strange experience reported by a psychiatrist by the name of Dr George Ritchie. The student, Raymond Moody, was attending the University of Virginia and was sitting with 20 or so others in a seminar given by Professor John Marshall; the subject of the seminar being philosophical issues related to death. Marshall told the group about a locally based psychiatrist who had been pronounced dead after a case of double pneumonia, and then successfully resuscitated. While he was 'dead', the psychiatrist had the remarkable experience of finding himself outside of his body. Marshall asked the students what this experience implied about the subjective nature of death

A few months later Moody had the opportunity to hear Dr Ritchie describe in person how in 1943 he had been in a hospital in Texas with a respiratory infection. Ritchie explained to the audience that at that time he was 20 years old and an army private. However, he was very excited because he had been selected to train as a doctor at the Medical College of Virginia. Unfortunately, this sudden illness was threatening to delay his enrolment at the college the following day, something that really concerned him. As he lay in bed something started to concern him more. He felt a swift rise in his temperature and then, to his horror, he began spitting up blood. As he leaned forward everything went black ... But only for a second or so.

Ritchie opened his eyes and discovered that he was lying in a strange bed. Looking around he found himself in a small, dimly lit, unfamiliar room and immediately assumed that he had fallen asleep and it was the next day, the day he had to travel to Richmond to enrol. In a panic he jumped out of bed fearing that he might miss his train. He looked back and froze. In a stunningly similar situation to my friend who phoned in to my radio programmes, he looked back to see a young man lying on the bed he had just vacated.

Concerned about missing the train, he turned round and walked into the corridor; as he did so he was approached by a ward boy. The boy ignored him, which was strange, but what happened next was even stranger. The young man walked straight through Ritchie and continued along the corridor. Totally shaken, Ritchie approached another man, a sergeant, carrying an instrument tray and asked him if he had seen the ward boy. The sergeant did not answer or show any sign that anyone was in front of him.

Before he had time to evaluate exactly what was happening, Ritchie found himself outside the hospital and flying through the air. Looking down he could see that he was still wearing his hospital pyjamas. Although quite well designed for a hospital ward, they were totally inadequate as protection from the cold night air. However, Ritchie felt no sensation of cold, only the feeling of moving very fast. He wondered if he could control his speed and, to his surprise, found that he could. He slowed himself down and manoeuvred himself to a soft landing on a street corner near a river. People were walking past him, but just as in the hospital they looked straight through him. Automatically he leaned against a thick guy-wire holding up a telegraph pole and was shocked as his body passed straight through it. He was later to write: 'In some unimaginable way I had lost my firmness of flesh, the body that other people saw.'

His major concern at this time was not how unusual his circumstances were, but that in this disembodied state a career as a doctor would be impossible. He knew that he had to return to the hospital as soon as possible and then, hopefully, find a way to get back into his physical body. He took to the air and in a flash he was back in the hospital. He had no idea in which ward his body was to be found. He ran from ward to ward, checking the sleeping faces of the soldiers. The light was dim which made identification really difficult. He then recalled that he owned a very distinctive fraternity ring made of gold and onyx. His search became more and more frantic. He then spotted the ring on the left hand of a body, but to Ritchie's horror this hand belonged to a body covered in a white sheet, clearly a very dead body. The young man realized that he, or at least his body, was dead. At that moment the whole room was filled with an intense light. This was the beginning of the second stage of Ritchie's NDE. In this phase Ritchie met a 'Being of Light' that he assumed to be Jesus. This being, after showing him many sights, told him that he had to return to his earthly life as it was not his time to die.

In a flash Ritchie found himself waking up in his earthly body. To his surprise he found himself under a white sheet, in exactly the same position that he saw himself to be before the Being of Light appeared. An orderly who had been preparing the body for the morgue noticed feeble signs of life in the corpse and called the doctor. The worried medic then hastily injected adrenaline directly into the heart. This jolted the young man into life – a second life. Although Ritchie had not taken a breath for nine full minutes, he showed no symptoms of brain damage. The commanding officer at the hospital was to describe the Ritchie case as 'the most amazing circumstance of my career' and was later to sign an affidavit that George Ritchie had indeed made a miraculous return from virtual death on that fateful night of 20 December 1943.

The implications of this case fascinated the young Raymond Moody and he decided to ask friends and acquaintances if they had experienced anything similar to that reported by Dr Ritchie, or indeed if they had heard of any similar cases. Much to his amazement Moody found that this phenomenon was far more common than he had expected. The reason why it was virtually unreported was because nobody had asked the question. For the next 11 years Moody amassed a huge collection of first-hand reports similar to that of George Ritchie. Indeed, what amazed Moody was just how consistent these reports seemed to be. He was sure that he had found something of profound significance. Such was his interest that after teaching philosophy for three years he decided that, although fascinating, it could not give him the answers he sought. He felt that the only way to really understand the meaning behind these experiences was to train as a doctor and test things out first-hand. Moody subsequently completed his degree in medicine and was to focus on the physiological as well as the psychological aspects of this unusual and unnamed phenomenon.

After collecting over 150 cases similar to that of George Ritchie's, Dr Moody decided to write a book about his findings. This book, *Life After Life* was an overnight bestseller. Considerable interest was generated by his book and soon other medical professionals became involved in collecting data and suggesting explanations for this intriguing phenomenon.

Although Moody was the first to announce to the world the existence of this experience, others were also working in the same area. One such researcher was Dr Karlis Otis and another was Dr Elizabeth Kubler-Ross. However, it was Moody who first pulled it all together under one readily recognizable term and acronym – the 'near-death experience', or NDE.

From his research Dr Moody was able to derive a set of nine traits that, for him, defined the NDE. He made it clear that not all subjects experience all nine, some may have only one or two. But, at least one must be present for the experience to be considered an NDE.

Moody's nine traits are:

- a sense of being dead
- peace and painlessness
- out-of-the-body experience
- the tunnel experience
- people of light
- rising rapidly into the heavens
- reluctance to return
- a past-life review
- an encounter with a supreme being of light

According to pollster George Gallop Jr, eight million adults in the United States have undergone a near-death experience. Of those responding to Gallop's questionnaire:

- 26 per cent reported the out-of-the-body sensation
- 9 per cent reported the tunnel experience
- 32 per cent had a life review
- 23 per cent sensed the presence of another being

What is interesting, but not part of Moody's 9 traits, is that 23 per cent of the respondents described heightened visual perceptions and 6 per cent claimed precognition.

Moody's book, backed up by statistics such as those presented by the Gallop Organization, was to bring about a considerable amount of interest within the medical profession. Dr Michael Sabom, a cardiologist, was keen to see if he could find any evidence for the NDE from his patients. Sabom was in a perfect position to check this out. He specialized in the resuscitation of patients who had suffered cardiac arrest. Sabom recognized the inherent difficulty of determining whether or not a resuscitated patient had been clinically dead. He carefully defined what criterion he would apply. This was 'any bodily state resulting from an extreme physiological catastrophe ... that would reasonably be expected to result in irreversible biological death in the majority of instances and would demand urgent medical attention'. Of the 78 patients interviewed by Sabom, 34 (43 per cent) reported an NDE. Applying Moody's nine traits the results were interesting:

- 92 per cent reported a sense of being dead
- 53 per cent reported the out-of-body experience
- 23 per cent described the tunnel experience
- 53 per cent experienced rising into the heavens
- 100 per cent reported a reluctance to return
- 48 per cent experienced a being of light

The other 'traits' not mentioned are individually included within the general definitions.

Interestingly, the Gallop survey suggests that 26 per cent of all near-death experiencers report an OBE. Michael Sabom's survey elicited an even higher number, 53 per cent.

A little-known classic NDE-related OBE was recorded by Mormon historian Bryant S Hinckley in his book *The Faith of our Pioneer Fathers*.[5] Published in 1956 this book describes the conditions and adversities endured by the Mormon pioneers as they crossed the American continent to found Salt Lake City. In this book Hinckley delves back into the letters and journals of these intrepid individuals. One such document describes how one of 'the Saints' was badly injured by a runaway wagon. Immediately after the incident the injured man found himself out of his body and looking down from above:

> His spirit left his body and stood, as it were, in the air
> above it. He could see his body and the men standing
> around and he heard their conversation. At his option

he could re-enter his body or remain in spirit. His
reflection upon his responsibility to his family and
his great desire to live caused him to choose to enter
his body again and live. As he did so he regained
consciousness and experienced severe pains incident
to the injuries which he had suffered in the accident.[6]

It appears that what we have is a seemingly consistent set of descriptions spanning many years. These people will not have heard of each
other nor, it is reasonable to conclude, would they have known about
how others perceived such an event when at the point of death. This
is clearly of significance. Whether this ecsomatic experience is a
complex hallucination engineered by the dying brain, or a genuine
out-of-body phenomenon is an open question. But one thing is for
sure. For those who experience such sensations, they are very real.

The Evidence

The historical cases discussed so far have involved subjective experiences of individuals who are close to death. In order to corroborate
what they saw in their out-of-body states, the experiencers returned
to their respective bodies and were able to describe their experiences subsequently to witnesses. However, there is one fascinating
historical case in which there was a 'real-death' experience.

Dr Josef Issels was one of the world's leading cancer specialists. In his later years he ran a clinic in the small Bavarian town of
Ringburg. Although a very controversial figure in the latter part of
his life, he ran a very sensitive and caring facility where terminally
ill patients were given hope that their disease could be cured. It was
one such patient who called Dr Issels into her room one morning.
She delightedly informed the surprised doctor that she could leave

her body at will. Although known for his unconventional views, the idea of out-of-the-body perception was not something that he believed in any way. Sensing his doubt the woman smiled and said to him 'I will give you proof, right here and now'. She told the incredulous Issels that he should immediately go down to Room 12 and that in the room he would find a woman writing a letter to her husband. 'She is on the first page', the patient stated, adding that 'I have just seen her do it'. Issels, playing along with her, rushed down to Room 12 which was located at the far end of the corridor. Walking into the room he was stunned to see a woman putting the final words on the first page of a letter. The woman further confirmed that it was a letter to her husband and that she had just started writing it a few minutes before.

Issels was amazed by this. He hurried back down the corridor to tell the astral-travelling patient that she was, indeed, correct. On entering the room he realized that between the time he left her room and his return the patient had died. Was her unusual ability related to the fact that she was about to die? Indeed, what is fascinating about this case was that the terminally ill woman did not experience an NDE. Her ability to leave her body was clearly related in some way to her impending death, but was not a part of the death process itself. What is even more intriguing is that this woman claimed that she could induce her out-of-the-body experiences by willing them to happen.

However, these cases are purely anecdotal. In recent years examples of what have been termed 'veridical' NDE-related OBEs have been reported. By the term 'veridical' it is meant that the images and incidents reported by the 'dying' person have subsequently been confirmed by others.

One of the all-time classic examples of a veridical NDE/OBE is the much quoted, and much analysed case known as 'Maria's Shoe'.

In April 1977 a female migrant worker was admitted into Seattle's Harborview Medical Centre in Washington State, USA. She had suffered a heart attack so was quickly rushed to the coronary care unit. She was in a very bad way and three days later she suffered a second, massive, heart attack. Fortunately, specialist staff were on hand and she was successfully resuscitated. Later that day a social worker called Kimberly Clark called in to check how 'Maria' was. Maria, although still ill, was very excited and keen to tell Clark that she had experienced a strange series of sensations whilst she was unconscious. She described how she witnessed her resuscitation from a position outside and above her body, noting printouts flowing from the monitoring machines measuring her vital signs. She then said that she became distracted by something over the area surrounding the emergency room entrance and 'willed herself' outside of the hospital. She accurately described the area surrounding the emergency room entrance, which Clark found curious since a canopy over the entrance would have obstructed Maria's view if she had simply looked out of her hospital-room window.

Floating in the air outside the window she spotted something strange on a third-floor window ledge at the far side of the hospital. Again she realized that she could 'will' herself to another location, as she suddenly found herself right next to the object that had caught her attention. It was a man's tennis shoe, specifically a dark-blue left-foot shoe with a worn-out patch over the little toe and a single shoelace tucked under its heel. With this image fresh in her mind she found herself back in her body as the crash team seemingly saved her life.

Clark was fascinated by this and agreed to try and see if Maria had actually seen something that existed outside her imagination. She walked outside the hospital, but could see nothing from ground level. She then re-entered the building and began a room-to-room search of the floor above the one where Maria's resuscitation took place. Clark could see nothing, even when pressing her head against the window to get a better view. Eventually, and to her great surprise, she did find the shoe. She entered one particular room on the third floor of the north wing and spotted the shoe, but from the vantage point inside the hospital she could not see the worn-out toe, which would have been facing outwards, or the tucked-in shoe lace.[7]

Later we shall discover that there is evidence to suggest that these cases are not quite as amazing as they seem when first encountered. Such criticisms have brought about a series of papers and counter-papers presented within the pages of the *Journal of Near-death Studies*. In one paper that appeared in the summer of 2007, Kimberley Clark, writing under her married name of Kimberley Clark Sharp, defended her position as reporter of the 'Maria' case. She remains adamant that Maria *did* see things that it was impossible for her to have known about unless she was floating outside of her body and looking down on the shoe.

The major problem with the 'Maria' case is that there is no confirmative information from any source other than Maria herself and the fact that the shoe was found to be in the location that Maria claimed it was. As we shall see later, there have been counter proposals put forward that the shoe could have been seen either from inside the hospital or from a location outside the building.

Another interesting case appeared in the highly respected medical magazine *The Lancet* in 2001:

> During night shift an ambulance brings in a 44-year
> old cyanotic, comatose man into the coronary care
> unit … . When we go to intubate the patient, he turns
> out to have dentures in his mouth. I remove these

upper dentures and put them onto the 'crash cart.' [...] Only after more than a week do I meet again with the patient, who is by now back on the cardiac ward. The moment he sees me he says: 'Oh, that nurse knows where my dentures are.' I am very surprised. Then he elucidates: 'You were there when I was brought into hospital and you took my dentures out of my mouth and put them onto that cart, it had all these bottles on it and there was this sliding drawer underneath, and there you put my teeth.[8]

In a subsequent paper on this case published in the Journal of *Near-death Studies*[9], Dutch researcher Rudolf H Smit discusses in great detail how this is a classic case of veridical perception during an NDE-induced OBE. The nurse's account was recorded on 2 February 1994 by a member of the Merkawah Foundation, a Dutch NDE research organization. In 12 closely typed pages the nurse gives a very detailed account of what took place that night. In fact, the male nurse found that the patient not only remembered the dentures being placed on the cart but also recounted, in great detail, conversations that had taken place between the nursing staff. The patient described how he had 'seen' everything from a position floating above the nursing staff and towards the corner of the room. However, a very curious comment was made by the patient in that, whilst he was floating outside of his body, he was also very aware of the pressure that his body was feeling as the crash nurse sat on top of it. He described how he felt 'enormous pain' when the heart massage machine was turned on. Although this sense of 'bi-location' should have felt very odd to the patient, the nurse reported that the patient 'told it so matter-of-factly, so down-to-earth' adding, 'He certainly was not a woolly thinking person, whose fantasy had run wild'.

This patient was reported as 'clinically dead' when he was brought into the hospital. In April 2008, many years after the event, another member of Merkawah, Titus Rivas, managed to trace the nurse and asked for further information regarding the incident. The nurse confirmed that the patient had been found unconscious in a field near the small village of Ooy, near Nijmegen. The night had been extremely cold and on arrival at the hospital it was reported that he had no heartbeat, no blood pressure was not breathing and his body was 'as cold as ice'. It was at this point that his dentures were removed, not later when he had started to recover.

Clearly this is a very powerful case and it does have certain parallels with another that was recorded as part of the 'Evergreen Study' into the NDE phenomenon in 1981 and conducted at the Evergreen State College in Washington State. In this case a woman who had suffered a ruptured Fallopian tube was rushed into an operating room to have an emergency procedure. A member of the medical team involved in the operation was her sister-in-law, a nurse. When the woman came round afterwards she described to her in-law that whilst unconscious she had experienced a very strange event. She found herself outside of her body looking down on the operating room. In a similar way to the Dutch cardiac patient, she was very aware of the events that were taking place below her viewpoint near the ceiling. She later described in detail what she perceived:

> I saw this little table over the operating table. You
> know, those little round trays like a dental office where
> they have their instruments and all? I saw a little tray
> like that with a letter on it addressed (from a relative
> by marriage she had not met).[10]

Unfortunately, the nurse herself was equally sure that there was neither a letter in the operating theatre nor, indeed, a round table.

However, it was later reported that there *was* a small rectangular table in the operating theatre. Technically this was not a table but a stand, in that a table has four legs whereas a stand sits on a tubular frame. These small tables are common features in operating theatres and dental practices across the world. The technical name for these devices is a 'Mayo Stand', called simply 'the Mayo' by medical staff. It was suggested by the Evergreen researchers that this may have been the source of the patient's confusion over the letter. It was highly likely that the operating theatre staff may have mentioned this stand as part of their discussions. It is reported that hearing is the last sense to shut down before death. As such, the patient's subconscious may have heard the word 'mayo' and perceived it to be a word that would be understood by a non-medical person. For example a comment like 'check the mayo' could have been interpreted as 'check the *mail*' or something similar.

Another case reported in the Evergreen Study shows exactly how an NDE-related OBE can involve non-veridical dream elements. After a car crash a woman found herself out of her body:

> Well, then I remember, not physical bodies but like
> holding hands, the two of us, up above the trees. It was
> a cloudy day, a little bit of clouds. And thinking here
> we go, we're going off into eternity ... and then bingo,
> I snapped my eyes open and I looked over and he was
> staring at me.[11]

Here we have the classical OBE sensation after an encounter with death, but within the OBE is a perception of another person that is sharing the experience. In this case the other person was also involved in the car crash and, if the evidence of the woman's senses is to be believed, was also floating above the accident. However, this was not the case and her male companion had not even lost consciousness.

In his fascinating article 'Hallucinatory Near-Death Experiences',[12] from which I take the above examples, writer Keith Augustine suggests that although there are many cases in which hallucinatory elements encroach into NDE-related OBEs, these cases are rarely reported by organizations such as IANDS or quoted within orthodox NDE books. He argues that this is because, in general, most NDE researchers are, in the final analysis, trying to show that there is a spiritual and non-materialistic element to the whole phenomenon.

Could it be that many, if not all, NDE-related OBEs can be explained in this way? Working on the assumption that dreams are a known phenomenon within the present scientific paradigm, and that a good deal of empirical research has suggested that the phenomenon known as *sleep paralysis* generates illusory OBEs, then this is a reasonable position to take. As we shall see later, sleep paralysis may be a clue to a fascinating and challenging neurological explanation for the whole phenomenon. This will suggest that the whole argument about whether consciousness is located within the brain or somewhere else is simply one of approach. For the time being the onus of proof has to lie with those who believe that this phenomenon presents evidence that perception can exist outside of the brain. And this is exactly what a series of experiments have endeavoured to prove over the last few years.

The Experiments

The author who first reported the Dutch 'dentures' case discussed above was Dr Pim van Lommel, a cardiologist based at the Rijnstate Hospital in Arnhem, Netherlands. Dr van Lommel and his associates

had interviewed 344 cardiac patients who were successfully resuscitated after cardiac arrest in 10 Dutch hospitals. Out of these patients,
62 reported an NDE, of whom 41 described a core experience.

Van Lommel is one of a new set of NDE researchers who, over
the last 20 years or so, have been attempting to find verifiable
evidence that the NDE-related OBE is a real, not hallucinatory,
experience.

One of original researchers taking this kind of approach, Dr
Janice Holden, Professor of Counseling and Interim Care of the
University of North Texas, has now been active in this field for
over 20 years, her first paper on the subject having been published
in 1988.[13]

This paper reported on the results of a questionnaire that Dr
Holden sent out to a sample of individuals who had reported OBEs
with strong visual perceptions while close to death.[14] In response
she received 63 usable replies. What these responses told her was
that OBE perceptions are very clear and detailed.

Within her sample, 79 per cent reported that the vision was
distortion-free, in colour, and involved a panoramic field of vision.
More importantly, 61 per cent claimed that their memory of the
event was crystal clear. This seems to conflict with the suggestion
that OBEs are a form of waking dream. Most people report dream
states to be confusing, fuzzy and difficult to remember in any great
detail. Indeed, 61 per cent claimed that they could read things
during their experience.

In 1990 Dr Holden published a paper with Leroy Joesten of the
Lutheran General Hospital at Park Ridge, Illinois. This was the first
recorded attempt, in controlled conditions, to test whether individuals in near-death states experience veridical perception. It is
clear that both Dr Holden and Chaplain Joesten are firm believers
in the 'spiritual' explanation of the NDE phenomenon, rather than

the materialistic, but this in no way clouded their judgement when evaluating the results of their experiment.

The experimenters placed visual targets in various locations around the Park Ridge Hospital. These included the emergency room, the coronary care unit and each room in the intensive care unit. These locations were:

> ... in the corners of hospital rooms in which
> near-death episodes were most likely to occur ... in
> such a way as to be visible only from a vantage point
> of looking down from the ceiling. No living person
> was to know the exact content of the stimuli, thus
> rendering the design double-blind. Once the patient
> was resuscitated from a near-death episode in one of
> the 'marked' rooms, knowledge of the content of the
> visual stimulus would be assessed.[15]

Their logic was simple. If a person perceives a genuine out-of-the-body experience during an NDE then they would be able to correctly identify the contents of the visual targets. Unfortunately, only one cardiac arrest took place in the entire 12-month period of the study. To make this even more frustrating, the patient was an Armenian immigrant with little English.

In 1994 a similar study took place at Hartford Hospital in Connecticut. The hospital's Director of Nursing, Madelaine Lawrence placed a scrolling LED display high on a cabinet located in the electrophysiology laboratory. This display was not visible to anyone standing up. As Lawrence stated, in order to see this somebody would have to 'use a ladder or be out of his body'. The LED display showed a randomly generated nonsense statement. The plan was that any patients who became unconscious during electrophysiology studies would be interviewed and asked to describe their experience.

By the end of the study three patients had reported the early stages of an OBE-like experience, but none moved far enough away from their body to see the sign.

Three years later a 12-month study was set up in the medical, emergency, and coronary care units of Southampton General Hospital in southern England. In this period, boards were suspended from the ceilings of the wards. Written on the ceiling-facing sides of the boards were various figures. These were not visible from the ground but would be in clear view of a disembodied consciousness floating near the ceiling itself. Of the 63 cardiac arrest survivors during that period, seven reported a level of awareness after they lost consciousness. Of these, four experienced NDE-type perceptions but none reported an OBE.

For her PhD thesis Penny Sartori of the Morrison Hospital in Swansea, Wales, placed randomized cards on top of the medical equipment within the resuscitation room of the hospital. This is the place where patients who have suffered a cardiac arrest are worked upon to save their lives. Because these monitors are above the eye level of a person standing up, they cannot be seen by anybody in the room. Sartori's idea was a simple one; if a patient had an OBE whilst 'dying' during a heart attack, it was possible that from an elevated and disembodied position they would see the cards and, hopefully, describe them if they survived the trauma. Sartori ran this experiment from January 1998 to January 2003.

During the period of her study, eight individuals reported NDE-related OBEs. None of them reported seeing the cards. According to a paper presented by psychiatrist Dr Peter Fenwick at the 2004 IANDS annual conference, this can be simply explained by the fact that during a traumatic NDE the patient will be more concerned about what was happening to them than spotting cards in odd places. He went on to describe how one experiencer looked at her body, then went out of the window; another described how she returned to her body as quickly as she could; and a third described how he went through a wall backwards. For Dr Fenwick, each of these circumstances was not conducive to a leisurely viewing of the environment within the resuscitation room.

In January 2004 Dr Holden decided to have a second attempt to finally prove that NDE/OBE perceptions can be shown to be true. She collaborated with Dr Bruce Greyson, Professor of Psychiatry at the University of Virginia and Dr J Paul Mounsey, Associate Professor of Internal Medicine, also at the University of Virginia. The three researchers had received a grant from the Portuguese Bial Foundation. The motivation for this research was made clear when the three described what they wished to demonstrate:

> ... patients during cardiac arrest have perceptions that
> they could not have had normally from the position
> of their bodies, [as this would provide profound]
> evidence for the independent functioning of the mind
> while the brain was physiologically impaired.[16]

The team decided to study such phenomena during the surgical implantation of cardioverter/defibrillators (ICDs). These are electrical devices that monitor the patient's heartbeat. If they detect a cardiac arrest they immediately administer an electric shock to return the heart to a normal rhythm. When these devices are implanted into a patient's chest, the surgeons deliberately induce a cardiac arrest to test the effectiveness and sensitivity of the ICD. When the cardiac arrest is induced, the patient enters a state exactly the same as that experienced during a natural heart attack. As such, they may experience an NDE and OBE. Unlike Lawrence's patients, all 25 individuals involved during the period of the study (January 2004 to July 2006) experienced at least 2 cardiac arrests during the procedure.

In these controlled conditions the experimenters had placed an opened laptop computer on top of either a cabinet or a video monitor. This ceiling-facing laptop computer was visible only from a perspective far above eye level. The laptop was programmed to generate easily recognized images such as a butterfly floating, a frog jumping, and fireworks exploding over the Statue of Liberty. Each image was displayed in red, orange, green or purple. The computer then followed a sequence of colours and lettering that lasted 40 seconds.

During the period, 52 patients were given induced cardiac arrests. Five patients acknowledged some recall of events while unconscious – such as a sense of timelessness, feelings of peace, vaguely being somewhere unfamiliar, and possibly sensing the presence of a deceased relative – but nothing resembling a full NDE or an OBE.

In his paper to the International Association of Near-Death Studies (IANDS) annual conference, Dr Peter Fenwick discussed why it was that after all these years, and many attempts, no clear proof of conscious awareness existing outside of the body has been found. Indeed, that is an understatement. As we have seen from our review of the papers, only the Penny Sartori experiment reported OBEs taking place in the controlled conditions. Despite years of experimental time, and many cardiac arrests, both induced and natural, no out-of-body experiences were reported in any of the other studies.

But Dr Fenwick was not disappointed by this; he was sure that proof of consciousness existing outside of the brain will soon be found. He stated that, in his opinion, the problem was the methodology. With this in mind he is now associated with another fascinating attempt to finally find his proof.

On 11 September 2008 a group of the world's leading researchers in this field met up at the United Nations Building in New York. Entitled *Beyond the Mind-Body Problem: New Paradigms in the*

Science of Consciousness, this symposium announced to the world that a new three-year study had been funded to finally prove, or disprove, the existence of near-death-experience-related out-of the-body experiences. The coordinator of this multi-national project would be Dr Sam Parnia, the physician behind the 1998 Southampton General Hospital research discussed above.

In many ways this project is similar to the one organized by Greyson and Holden. Special shelving will be placed in resuscitation areas within 25 hospitals across the United Kingdom, the United States and Europe. These shelves will hold pictures, but these pictures will only be visible from the ceiling. Dr Parnia has clearly set out exactly what the object of this study will be. During the launch of the 'AWARE' (AWAreness during REsuscitation) Study he stated:

> If you can demonstrate that consciousness continues
> after the brain switches off, it allows for the possibility
> that the consciousness is a separate entity. It is unlikely
> that we will find many cases where this happens, but
> we have to be open-minded. And if no one sees the
> pictures, it shows these experiences are illusions or
> false memories. This is a mystery that we can now
> subject to scientific study.[17]

Clearly Dr Parnia and his associates do not share Dr Fenwick's concern with the methodology. However, it does seem that this is simply doing exactly the same work as Greyson and Holden did between 2004 and 2006, the only difference being that there is much greater public knowledge about this project, together with a similarly inflated level of expectation. At the time of the writing this book (November 2010), nothing has been reported either in the specialist journals or the general media as to how this project is progressing. I can only assume from the lack of dramatic announcements that, just like all the other attempts, the AWARE study has drawn a huge zero as regards any scientific evidence for veridical perceptions during a near-death experience.

Interestingly enough, this project, and all the previous attempts, contradicts a long-held assumption that people in out-of-body states can neither read things nor perceive numbers, because it is exclusively the non-dominant hemisphere (usually the right) that is active during such events. This has been used many times as a way of explaining why all such experiments set up to prove veridical OBEs have failed.

In using this excuse, those who believe that the body and mind are separate entities need to be very careful. A sceptic will, not unreasonably in my opinion, reply that it is not the methodology that is at fault as it confirms what many others have long suggested – that the OBE is simply an hallucination. A zero return on any of the experiencers seeing the cards in the Penny Sartori experiment is exactly what such an assumption would suggest. They did not see the cards because they were not outside their body at the time. It will be interesting to see if, as I suspect, a similar zero response is reported at the end of the AWARE study.

However, there does seem to be one area of evidence that curiously uses the absence of sight to prove that the NDE-related OBE is a very real phenomenon – the near-death experiences of blind people. It is to this challenging area that we now turn.

The Challenge of the Blind NDE

All the OBE cases discussed above involve sensory perception that is being supplied by an unknown process. How can a person 'see' and 'hear' things when they have no eyes to see or ears to hear? Indeed, the mystery of how this process works deepens when one considers that there is no physical brain to present this information to consciousness. If veridical OBEs are real, and not simply hallucinatory states, then our understanding of how the brain works is in error. This is not a small error but something that would demand a radical reassessment of everything we have learned from neurology and physiology. In this scenario the brain is not the location of consciousness and, even more amazing, consciousness does not need the physical body to continue existing.

Modern science will need more than the evidence presented by subjective experiences in order to test this. As has been stated many times, the plural of anecdote is not evidence. However, there is one specific area of veridical OBE research that is very difficult to dismiss as hallucination. This involves the near-death experiences of blind people who, in the OBE state, claim that they can see.

The NDE researcher Kenneth Ring identified 21 blind individuals who had experienced an NDE. Of these, 10 had been born blind, 9 had lost their sight before the age of 5 and 2 were severely visually handicapped. Interestingly, 10 of the subjects claimed that they 'saw' their body below them during the NDE. These 10 all reported the usual Moody traits including the flying down the tunnel towards a bright light and having an encounter with a being of light.[18] One of the most interesting subjects was a 43-year-old called Vicki Umipeg.

Vicki had been born extremely prematurely and too much oxygen had been given to her after her birth. This destroyed her optic nerve. As a result of this miscalculation she had been blind since birth. During her life Vicki had suffered two NDEs. The first was when she was 20 and was brought about by an attack of appendicitis. However, it was the second that is of great interest. She was involved in a car crash when she was 22. In her NDE she 'saw' herself as she hovered above the hospital bed and noticed that a section of her very long hair had been shaved off. After this she felt herself float through the roof and then saw streetlights and houses below her. She then found herself in a field covered with flowers. In this field were people she had known who were long dead. Suddenly a radiant figure walked towards her. She took this figure to be Jesus, although he never identified himself as such. This Being of Light gave her a full 'Life Review' that she saw in colour and in great detail. After this the being told her she must return in order to 'bear her children'. This greatly excited Vicki because at that time motherhood was only a dream. With this she found herself slammed back into her body and experienced once more the heavy dullness and intense pain of her physical being.[19]

What may be of general significance is the fact that Vicki now has three children.

This case, and the others presented by Kenneth Ring and his co-writer Evelyn Elsaesser-Valarino (the researcher who introduced me to Engelbert Winkler and Dirk Proeckl) in their book *Lessons from the Light,* suggests that there is another way in which the mind can process sensory stimulation that does not involve an embodied brain or an eye. Again we will discuss a possible explanation for Vicki's fascinating experience in a later chapter, and explanations for cases such as these are needed if our present scientific paradigm is to hold firm.

A near-death experience takes place during a particularly stressful and disturbing time. It is not really surprising that in such a state unusual psychological perceptions manifest. Indeed, it has been suggested by some researchers that the whole NDE is simply a brain-generated illusion to help the dying person cope with the distress and trauma. However, the out-of-body experience is not isolated to such circumstances. As we shall discover in the next few chapters, for certain individuals the popping in and out of the soma can become a way of life. This was certainly the case for probably the most famous of all 'astral travellers', American businessman Robert Monroe. It is to his fascinating story that we now turn our attention.

CHAPTER 4

A Special Case:
Robert Monroe

The Early Experiences

Robert Monroe is probably the most famous of the modern astral travellers. Monroe was born in 1915 and grew up in Lexington, Kentucky. Up until 1958 he led a very normal life. Initially he worked within the radio and television industry and then, later in his career, he made a very successful move into advertising. However, one Sunday in the spring of 1958 his life was to change forever. His family had gone to church leaving Robert alone at home. He took the opportunity to test out something that he had long planned to do. As somebody who had worked in the radio industry for many years, he was interested in the effect that background sound had on concentration. Through his tape sound system he played one sound signal whilst attempting to block out all other sensory input. His plan was to try and recall later all the things he thought about in this isolated state.

His family returned and they all had brunch. Just over an hour later, Robert was overcome by an intense pain in his stomach. As no other member of his family was affected by this unpleasant sensation he came to the conclusion that it must have been as a direct result of his earlier experiment. The pain continued unabated for hours until, at midnight, he fell asleep exhausted.

The next morning the pain and cramps had gone, but Robert was convinced that something within him had changed. He was later to describe this as 'the touch of a magic wand'.

Three weeks later he was again alone on a Sunday afternoon. He was lying down on the couch in his living room when something very strange happened. He saw a beam or ray come out of the sky to the north. The beam then hit him and suffused his body with warmth. Indeed, had he not been looking north he would have assumed it was sunlight. What happened next assured him that whatever the beam was, it certainly was not a sunbeam. His entire body started shaking violently. He felt himself vibrating all over and he realized that he could not move. After a short time he managed to free himself from this vice-like grip and as he did so the vibration slowly faded away. As far as he was aware he had not lost consciousness but he knew that something very odd had happened. For some reason he felt that this odd event was linked to the sickness he had experienced a few weeks before. Over the next six weeks the same peculiar condition manifested itself nine times. Clearly there was something very peculiar going on. The one consistency seemed to be that it always manifested just as he was resting or about to fall asleep. On one occasion the vibration developed into a ring of sparks, about two feet in diameter, that encircled his body. It would start at his feet and work its way up his body to his head. When it eventually reached his head he felt a great surge of energy and a roaring sound. What is intriguing is that Robert could only see the ring of sparks when he closed his eyes. This was all very peculiar, but a few months later things were to become stranger still.

As he was dozing one evening the vibrations returned. By this stage he had become so used to them – bored even – he patiently waited for them to subside so he could go off to sleep. As he lay waiting he realized that his arm was draped out of the bed, brushing the top of the rug with his fingertips. He realized that he could move his fingers so he decided to scratch the rug. After a second or so something strange happened; his fingers went through the rug and he felt the surface of the wooden floor beneath. Intrigued, he pushed further and his fingers went through the floor and into the room below. Curiously, his semi-conscious mind did not find this particularly odd. He continued pushing and soon his whole arm was in the room below. He then felt his fingers touch water. Absent-mindedly playing with the surface of the water he suddenly became fully aware of the situation; being wide awake, eyes open, but yet he could still feel the water playing round his fingertips. He pulled his hand back into the room and checked his fingers. He was expecting to see traces of water on them; there were none. He looked down at the floor; there was no hole. Eventually he calmed down and went to sleep.

Clearly, this was a very disturbing dream. He discussed it with his doctor who agreed it was odd but offered no explanation. Four weeks later the vibrations returned, and this time Robert Monroe's world-view was to be changed forever.

He was again lying in bed, his wife asleep next to him. The vibrations started and Robert tried to take his mind off what was taking place. Monroe was a keen flyer and a later psychological profile was to show that he had been fascinated by flight ever since he was a child. As such, he thought about how nice it would be to take a glider up into the sky and float around on the thermals, making a mental note to do this the next day. Obviously, something had subliminally placed this image in his mind, evidenced by what happened next.

As he thought about the flight, he felt something pressing against his shoulder. Putting his hand out to find out what this was, he encountered a smooth wall; his hand followed the surface, which continued smooth and unbroken. Opening his eyes, in the dim light he could see that he was lying on his side on what he at first assumed to be the wall next to his bed. His natural thought was that he had somehow fallen out of bed and onto the floor. However, as he looked up he could see no windows or doors. It felt both strange and yet familiar. And then he realized why. It wasn't the wall but the ceiling! He felt himself gently bouncing on and off the ceiling. He was then able to roll his body round to look down, and saw in the dim light his bed. Lying in the bed asleep were two figures. With amazement he realized that one was his wife and the other was ... himself.

It then dawned on him. He had died. What other explanation could there be for him being outside of his body. He panicked and swooped down to the bed and dived back into his body. Cautiously he opened his eyes to find himself back within his own flesh. The vibrations faded away. He was so stunned at this, all he could think of doing was lighting a cigarette and looking out of the window, hoping that the nicotine and the view would help explain what he had just experienced.

Discovering the Locales

The above events were described in great detail in a book that Robert was subsequently to write describing his experiences. First published in 1971, this book, entitled *Journeys Out of the Body*, was to become a bestseller. People took to it because Monroe was clearly a grounded individual who had had a successful career as a business executive and president of a multimillion-dollar business. He had no financial need to write such a book and his descriptions had the ring of sincerity. Robert was to continue in his job with the support of his associates who were also fascinated by the implications of his experiences, particularly with regard to how events developed after his first ecsomatic experience.

Not surprisingly this experience really worried Monroe. He went to see his doctor friend, who suggested that he was working too hard and maybe he should cut down on his smoking. And that was it. A visit to another friend, a psychologist this time, also failed to give him any answers.

However, the vibrations continued, but Robert was not keen to repeat the out-of-body exercise. This is interesting because it suggests that Robert had realized that, although he could not control the vibrations, he could will himself out of his body. In the book he fails to explain how he came to this knowledge, but he is quite specific that it was at his choosing when the next ecsomatic experience took place. He describes it in this way:

> With the vibrations in full force, I thought of floating upward – and I did. I smoothly floated up over the bed, and when I willed myself to stop, I did, floating in mid-air. It was not a bad feeling at all, but I was nervous about falling suddenly. After a few seconds I thought myself downward, and a moment later I felt myself in bed again with all normal physical senses fully operating. There had been no discontinuity in consciousness from the moment I lay down in bed until I got up after the vibrations faded. If it wasn't real – just hallucination or dream – I was in trouble. I couldn't tell where wakefulness stopped and dreaming began.[20]

I find the last line of crucial importance. Robert acknowledges that he is not sure if these are dreams or reality. Could they be both – a lucid dream, perhaps?

From that time onwards Robert had many similar experiences. These included some fascinating incidents that seemed to be taking place in another location to that of the everyday world encountered in a normal, fully awakened state – there were encounters with other beings that were clearly self-motivated entities with individual personalities. As time went on, Robert found that his out-of-body adventures were taking place in a series of totally different environments. He called these places 'Locales' and eventually concluded that there were three that could be encountered when journeying outside of the body.

The first of these, Locale 1, corresponds more or less to the normal physical world. The geography and inhabitants are generally identical to the everyday world. This is the Locale that Robert first encountered when he found himself floating near the ceiling of his bedroom. What he saw was from an odd angle but was understandable to him. Travels in this Locale can supply veridical information that can be reported back after the experience is finished. Robert gives a few examples of this including an attempted 'visit' he made to the home of a close friend, Dr Bradshaw, whilst in an ecsomatic state. He knew that Bradshaw was ill and was keen to see how he was. He found his journey was far more difficult than he had anticipated. Curiously, 'travelling' up the hill to the part of town where Bradshaw lived was *extremely* difficult. Why this should be is unclear, particularly as Monroe was, I assume, flying above the ground and, as such, an incline of any sort should not be an obstacle. Of course if he was walking in his ecsomatic state then climbing a hill may be a problem. Suffice to say, what happened was even more peculiar. Robert felt that someone or something lifted him up under each arm and helped him on his way. This was Robert's first encounter with the entities that seem to inhabit the ecsomatic universe. When he eventually arrived at the house he was puzzled to see that Dr Bradshaw and his wife were outside taking a walk. Robert tried in vain to attract their attention:

> I floated around in front of them, waving, trying to get their attention, without result. Then without turning his head, I thought I heard Dr Bradshaw say to me, 'Well, I see you don't need help anymore'. Thinking I had made contact, I dove back into the ground and returned to the office, rotated my body and opened my eyes.[21]

Robert describes how he later phoned Mrs Bradshaw, who confirmed that at the time of Robert's 'visit' she and her husband had been walking outside their house. Robert asked her what she was wearing. What she described was exactly what Robert had seen in his ecsomatic state.

This particular incident has been cited by Robert and his supporters as the first proof that Robert actually perceived things he could not know of by normal means. Indeed, many state that this was veridical evidence of Robert's ecsomatic state. Unfortunately I do not share that opinion. For example, we only have Robert's perception of the events; neither Dr Bradshaw nor his wife confirmed in any way that anything unusual happened during their walk. Robert describes how Dr Bradshaw spoke to him in a way that suggested he had seen him; later, Dr Bradshaw stated that he had not seen Robert nor spoken to him. However, Robert did correctly describe what the couple were wearing, which is very impressive. The question remains though, as to why Robert effectively 'distance viewed' but did not manage to have any physical effect upon the environment. I find this half-and-half situation of great significance.

The Tests

To assist us in understanding Robert's skills we have a series of well-documented experiments that took place under the guidance of Monroe's friend, Dr Charles Tart, in July 1966. Dr Tart used the facilities of the electroencephalographic laboratory of the University of Virginia Medical School.

Robert was in an isolation room with electrodes placed upon his head and devices in his ears to block out sound. He was asked to try and induce an ecsomatic experience and then read a five-digit target number which had been placed on a shelf, six feet above the floor. We will encounter a similar experiment also carried out by Dr Tart in a later chapter. In order to induce a sleep-like state, Robert was lying on a cot.

In his first book, Robert describes in some detail how this experiment was experienced from his point of view. He explains how a sense of warmth flooded through his body and took this as a cue to try what he termed 'the roll-out method'. This simply involves turning the 'astral body' onto the side, as one would do with the physical body when getting out of bed. Robert felt himself roll out of his body and out of the cot. He braced himself to hit the floor; when it didn't happen he knew that he was fully out of his body. He termed this state 'disassociated'. He moved through a darkened area, and then saw three people: two were male and one was female. The woman was tall and dark-haired and Robert suggested that she was probably in her 40s. She was sitting on a couch. Standing either side of her were two men, and the group was involved in conversation. Robert decided he needed to make his presence felt, so he moved forward and pinched the woman gently on her left side, just below her ribs. He felt that she reacted to this in some way.

Robert was slightly disappointed by this, so he decided to go back 'to the physical' as he termed it. He waited a few minutes and then moved out of his body for a second time. Using the same roll-out technique he exited his body and followed the light coming down from the corridor. He tried to find the technician but she was not in the control-console room. He then moved out into a brightly lit outer room and spotted her with another man who was standing to her left. What happened then was rather odd. Monroe describes it in this way:

> I tried to attract her attention, and was almost
> immediately rewarded with a burst of warm joy and
> happiness that I had finally achieved the thing we had
> been working for. She was truly excited, and happily
> and excitedly embraced me. I responded, and only
> slight sexual overtones were present, which I was
> about 90 per cent able to disregard. After a moment,
> I pulled back, and gently put my hands on her face,
> one on each cheek, and thanked her for her help.[22]

He then tried to attract the man's attention but failed; the pinching approach again received no reaction. He described the man as being about the same height as the technician and with curly hair. Robert then decided to return to his body. On doing so he called the technician and when she came into the room he told her that he had been successful in his attempt to get out of his body and that he had seen her with another man. She confirmed that indeed she had been in the outer room with another man – her husband had called by to see her. Robert asked to meet him, and recognized the curly-haired man he had seen in his ecsomatic state.

The 'communication' between Robert and the lab technician during his ecsomatic state has some parallels with his earlier encounter with Dr Bradshaw. You will recall that Robert was sure that his friend had both seen and spoken to him when he 'visited' him at his house, but Dr Bradshaw had no such perceptions and recalled no communication of any sort.

Quite naturally both Monroe and Tart were somewhat disappointed with this result. Unfortunately, Tart was soon to leave the University of Virginia where the experiments had taken place and move to a new post at a university in California. However, after moving into his new house, Tart decided that this could be used as a test of Monroe's ability to 'astral travel'. Tart telephoned Monroe in Virginia and suggested that he would, with the assistance of his wife Judy, create a 'psychic beacon' whereby they could guide Monroe's astral body to their new home in California. The test would determine if Monroe could describe a place he had never seen.

On the day of the experiment Tart telephoned Monroe. All he told him was that at some time during that evening he and Judy would start the process. At 11:00pm Californian time they began. This was 2:00am local time for Monroe in Virginia. Their plan was to continue concentrating until 11:30pm. Five minutes into the exercise their phone rang; this was not only annoying for them as it broke into their concentration, but also highly unusual. They let it ring. Eventually the caller gave up. As they had no answer-phone facility at that time, they had no idea who the caller was. They continued concentrating until 11:30 and then retired.

The next day Tart telephoned Monroe and stated that, in his opinion, the experiment had gone well and requested that Monroe send his description of what he experienced the previous night. A few days later the letter arrived.

Both Tart and his wife were intrigued to discover that the mystery caller on the night of the experiment had been Monroe himself. At around 2:00am he had been lying in bed and was wide-awake. He suddenly felt a rocking sensation then a tugging at his feet. He then felt a hand take his wrist and pull him out of his body. Feeling a rush of air for about five seconds, he then found himself inside a room.

After a brief ecsomatic experience Monroe described how he found himself back in his body in Virginia. He arose and immediately phoned the Tarts in California. His experience had taken around five minutes of 'external' time.

On the face of it this is a fascinating case. At exactly the moment Judy and Charley start to concentrate on bringing Robert to their home in California, Robert feels that he is being pulled out of his body, the timing being confirmed by the telephone conversation the following morning. This was not the main aim of the experiment, however. The plan was to see if Monroe could identify the layout of the new house in California and, by doing so, prove veridical perception. Dr Tart does not describe this in his article, but does make the following comment:

> The portion of his account that I have omitted, on the other hand, his description of our home and what my wife and I were doing, was quite inaccurate. He perceived too many people in the room, and perceived my wife and me performing actions that we did not do. Looking at the description, I would conclude that nothing psychic had happened.[23]

Dr Tart's final attempt to obtain veridical proof of Monroe's claimed abilities took place in 1968. Yet again this proved to be disappointing. Monroe was rigged up with various measuring devices and, for the first time, he was observed on a closed-circuit television screen for one of his claimed out-of-body experiences. Dr Tart was hoping to record Monroe's 'astral body' as it floated out of his physical body.

Dr Tart had requested that, whilst in his out-of-body state, Robert should make his way to another room in the laboratory where a five-digit number had been written down in a place of prominence. This was a format that Tart was to use in a later experiment, and, it must be said, with far greater perceived success.

In his first out-of-body state Monroe found himself in the hall between the two rooms, but because of 'breathing difficulties', as he described them, he could only linger in the ecsomatic state for 8 to 10 seconds. This puzzles me, yet in his discussion of the experiment Dr Tart makes no comment on this curious problem. If Monroe was in his 'astral body' why would he need oxygen? Or was it that his physical body was having breathing problems? If so, how did he know? Does this suggest that he was in some form of bi-location or is it evidence that his ecsomatic experiences had a far more complex, and ultimately far more challenging, cause?

At his second attempt Monroe decided to follow the EEG cable through the wall into the equipment room. I can only assume that he was trying to minimize the time he was 'out-of-body' because of his previous breathing problems. In doing so he managed to get lost and found himself facing a wall of another building, later identified as a courtyard opposite the equipment room. Curiously, many subsequent reports of this experiment consider it to be a success and a vindication of Monroe's astral-travelling abilities.

Dr Tart had three attempts at showing that Robert's skills were real and on each occasion the results were, at best, inconclusive. It is clear from the writings of Dr Tart, both at the time and subsequently, that he wanted to believe that Monroe could see things from an out-of-the-body location. But the experimental evidence suggests otherwise. Indeed it is interesting to note that the vague successes of the experiments (the waking up at the right time and the identification of the courtyard) are not in any way conclusive (it is possible that Robert could have seen the courtyard using normal vision, for example) and these 'hits' were not actually part of the controlled experiments.

However, there may be a perfectly reasonable explanation as to why Robert consistently failed to provide irrefutable evidence of veridical perceptions during his ecsomatic journeys. This explanation is hinted at in all of his books and is supported by the neurological evidence that I will present in a later chapter. It is to do with his concept of 'Locales'.

You will recall that earlier I described Monroe's 'Locale 1' as being geographically identical to our everyday world. This is, to all intents and purposes, the 'real world'. When travelling in an ecsomatic state in this Locale, Monroe suggests that veridical information can be gleaned and presented to the researchers as proof of the ecsomatic experience. This is the place where Robert believed he was in each of the experiments and experiences that have been described in this chapter; but as Robert describes in his books there are two other 'Locales'. Not surprisingly he calls these 'Locale 2' and 'Locale 3'.

It is in these two Locales that Robert spends the majority of his time for the rest of his first book. Indeed, his second book, *Far Journeys*, only really discusses Locale 3.

Monroe describes Locale 2 as being a further step away from ordinary reality. This is the place where heaven and hell can be found, meaning that the structure and inhabitants of this place are influenced by the hopes and fears of the experiencer. It seems to be the place where the subconscious becomes real. Of course, one could draw parallels here with ordinary dreaming, which also contains archetypes and symbols drawn from the depths of the human psyche.

Nevertheless, Monroe is sure that the beings encountered in Locale 2 are real. Not only that, but these beings 'create' an environment that will be familiar to any 'travellers' who may find themselves there during an out-of-body experience. In traditional occult lore

Locale 1 has been known by the terms of the lower astral plane. Monroe agrees with the occultists that the lower planes – those nearest to Locale 1 – are inhabited by potentially hostile entities and they should be traversed with care; Locale 2 can sometimes be negotiated with the help of the benign inhabitants of this region. For want of a better term Monroe calls these beings 'Helpers'. However they are not always around and indeed some of the more malign beings may disguise themselves to fool unwary travellers. In keeping with both occult lore and modern psychology, he suggests that Locale 2 is the place we all go in dreams; in which case, if the dreamer becomes 'lucid' whilst dreaming, then they will be able to manipulate Locale 2 to their own advantage. As this control is very limited the traveller needs to be wary. Of course, this is the phenomenon known as 'lucid dreaming', a topic I will return to later.

For me, however, it is Locale 3 that is the most significant place that Robert Monroe encountered.

Locale 3: Monroe's Shamanic Journey?

How Monroe first encountered this place is the most singular section of *Journeys Out of the Body*. As we have seen, Monroe used something he termed 'the roll-out technique' to move from everyday reality into Locale 1, but one evening in November 1958, instead of rolling through 90 degrees and exiting his body, he found that his 'rotation' continued to 180 degrees. He found himself 'face down', in the direct opposite position to his physical body. What he encountered there was totally bizarre:

> There was a hole. That is the only way to describe it.
> To my senses, it seemed to be a hole in a wall which
> was about two feet thick and stretched endlessly in all
> directions (in the vertical plane).[24]

He looked into the hole and saw nothing but the deepest blackness, but was sure that if his vision was good enough he would have seen stars and planets – believing that it was a part of deepest space. He then rotated back through the 180 degrees and returned to regular reality.

The following week he encountered the 180-degree turn again and, as expected, there was the hole. This time he placed a hand into the darkness and was astounded when another hand appeared and shook it! What was even stranger, when he put his hand in again the other hand gave him a business card with a New York address on it. Unfortunately Robert never mentions this card again. It would be fascinating to know if he followed up the address and what he discovered. Indeed, if he did keep this card it would be an artefact from another level of reality.

Over a period of weeks Robert eventually managed to get through the hole and encountered a world much like our own but with curious differences. For example, the technology seemed slightly unusual with different automobile design. He managed to explore this new world and was surprised to discover that there was a version of him that exists in this alternative Earth. He called this person 'I There' and, without his control, he found himself taking over the body of 'I There' for short periods of time. This caused profound problems for Robert and, one can only assume, great difficulty for 'I There' who must have experienced these things like petit mal 'absences'. Yet again we have a temporal lobe epilepsy parallel within a parallel universe. The implications of Robert's first encounters with Locale 3, as he subsequently termed this place, are of great significance for my own hypothesis about the nature of reality.

The 'Helpers' were of great importance when Robert was in Locale 3. It seems that whilst in this Locale he has just one, a being that seems to know considerably more about Monroe than should have been the case. Clearly, this being shares his life in all Locales including everyday reality. In an incident recorded as having taken place in March 1959, Robert was lying in bed when the usual vibrations started. By now he had become used to his journeys to Locale 3 and wished to know why this was happening and what it was all for. He saw a white ray of light appear and focus on his head. He decided that now was the moment to ask his question. As he did so, something very peculiar happened:

> A rich, deep voice – yet not a voice, and certainly not my conscious mind, as I was waiting expectantly – answered.
>
> 'Are you sure you want to know?' It came more from the light ray.
>
> I replied that I was sure.
>
> 'Are you strong enough to take the true answers?' There was little inflection and no emotion in the delivery.
>
> I replied that I thought I was. I waited and it seemed a long time before the voice spoke again.
>
> 'Ask your father to tell you of the great secret.'[25]

Just at that moment a member of his family came up the stairs and switched on a light outside his bedroom; with that the ray of light faded and Robert could not get it back. This was to be the last time that he communicated with this being. He asked his father the question, as suggested by the voice, but he was of no help. What this signifies is quite a mystery, but one that reminds me greatly of a similar incident reported by the science fiction writer Philip K Dick. This also involved a mysterious light source and an entity that guided and made suggestions. (This is discussed in detail in the last chapter of my book *The Daemon – A Guide To Your Extraordinary Secret Self*.)

In his last two books Monroe seems to focus almost totally on Locale 3 and how this can be visited by using something he called 'hemispheric synchronization' or 'HemiSync®'. Those who have followed on his work, such as Tom Campbell, continue to focus in on this particular place. It is as if the seeming failures encountered when testing veridical perception in Locale 1 forced Monroe to focus more on the 'Far Journeys' into Locale 3. A sceptic may observe that this was because journeys into Locale 3 cannot, by their very nature, be verified experimentally. I am not of that opinion. I believe that what Robert Monroe experienced was very real, possibly even more real than the normal world below Locale 1. Furthermore, I believe that all of Robert's ecsomatic experiences took place in Locale 3 and that is why he failed to prove he had the power of 'remote viewing'.

Nevertheless, others seem determined to believe that ecsomatic perception can occur within the physical world. In his introduction to Monroe's first book, *Journeys Out of the Body*, Dr Charles Tart presents a classic example of this counterproductive wishful thinking. From the evidence above, it is reasonable to state that not one of his experiments with Monroe presents any real proof that Monroe was travelling outside of his body in Locale 1. For example, in one experiment Monroe claimed that he had to return to his body because he had 'difficulty breathing'. He finds this hard to understand. I can only assume that in some way during his ecsomatic state, Monroe was both aware of his corporeal body lying on the bed in the experiment room whilst at the same time viewing the world through his astral body. This suggests some form of bi-location or else a doubling of consciousness. But even if we accept this, why was it that a difficulty in breathing was a problem? In his later journeys in Locale 2 and Locale 3, Monroe never mentions any corporeal body 'feedback'. Indeed, as far as I am aware this is the only time that Monroe mentions this as a problem. But I am more confused as to what brought about this 'difficulty in breathing'. In my experience I have never been woken from a dream because I could not breathe. I can only assume that Monroe's problem was that his corporeal body was forced to lie in an unnatural position and this caused some form of distress. But by accepting this we have to further accept that there is a non-local form of communication that takes place between the astral body and the corporeal body. Within the 'normal' world two objects cannot communicate unless they are in contact in some way or another. So, by what unknown mechanism does the astral body receive information from its corporeal body? During this time it is assumed that both bodies were within a few metres of each other; by implication the communication of distress was instantaneous. As such, it matters little whether the distance was 10 metres or 10 light-years. In a later chapter we will encounter scientifically verified phenomena which may help explain what was happening to Robert at that time.

I am keen to follow this to its logical conclusion. The implication is that if Monroe was aware of his breathing difficulty, then his astral body must have been aware of the breathing process. Although this is controlled by the autonomic nervous system it can be overridden by consciousness. Does this imply that the astral body is both fully aware of what is happening to the corporeal body, as well as being able to influence the actions of the corporeal body at a distance? Again, how does this work?

Let me suggest an alternative explanation. Could it simply be that Monroe was immediately aware of his breathing problems because he was within his body all the time? This would certainly explain it. Prosaic, I know, but nevertheless also quite reasonable when taking into account his inability to report anything vaguely veridical.

In my previous books I have written extensively about temporal lobe epilepsy and how this 'altered state' can open consciousness to other levels of reality. I am of the opinion that Robert may have been experiencing something similar – either that or a classic migraine. My reasons for this suspicion are that Monroe himself considered this option and dismissed it because, as he understood it, epilepsy was inherited and manifested at an early age, and that 'epileptics have no memory or sensation in such seizures'. Monroe is wrong on both counts. In some cases epilepsy does run in families, but it also can be instigated by scars (lesions) on the brain that can be caused by accidents or damage due to illness. More importantly, epileptics whose 'illness' is focused on the temporal lobes usually experience something called the 'aura'. This involves unusual perceptions and feelings that act as an 'early warning system' that a seizure is imminent.

I am fascinated that Monroe describes the sensation before he had his first ecsomatic experience as being like a vibration that ran through his body, likening it to a painless electric shock.[26] This is very similar to the aura of both migraine and temporal lobe epilepsy. I am aware that Robert states that he was tested for any neurological issues but I wonder what they actually looked for when they did these tests. Indeed, Robert manifested many other symptoms of the 'aura state'. He heard voices such as those of the 'Helpers', and the amazing encounter with the 'talking light' discussed earlier. My research suggests that these encounters are not simply hallucinations brought about by faulty brain chemistry, but are actually glimpses into an alternative reality facilitated by that brain chemistry.

The second half of this book will attempt an explanation for what may have been taking place in Robert's brain during his ecsomatic adventures. However, before we start on the science I would like to spend the next chapter looking at the skills of another very famous 'traveller', the 'distance viewer' Ingo Swann.

CHAPTER 5

Remote Viewing: The Case of Ingo Swann

Swann's Way

A careful review of the ecsomatic experiences of Robert Monroe will suggest that he was not really travelling outside of his body as much as viewing places and people from a distance. It was as if his consciousness left his body and bi-located itself somewhere else. Remote viewing is a related but qualitatively different phenomenon; a 'skill' that was to become in great demand during the days of the Cold War and one of the most famous practitioners of this skill was the artist Ingo Swann.

According to his own accounts Ingo Douglas Swann (or Swan, as his surname was at the time) first experienced an ecsomatic experience when he was two years old. He had just become unconscious after being given ether before an operation to have his tonsils out. The next thing he knew he was looking down at the scene from a location near the ceiling. He could see a table and a man leaning over a little body. The man was clearly having difficulty with something. In his irritation the surgeon swore as he struggled to cut something in the mouth of the little patient, unconscious on the table. Even at such an early age Ingo realized that this was odd. He was very aware that the body on the table was his own, but he was no longer in that body. Swann described how he felt – like being a point of awareness viewing the doctor's difficulties from a few feet away and from an elevated position. He saw the surgeon's knife cut into his tongue and was disturbed when the surgeon removed two pink and bloody lumps of flesh, placed them in a bottle and gave it to a nurse. The nurse then put the bottle on a sideboard behind two rolls of tissue.

The next thing Swann recalled was waking up. His mother was there to comfort him and at her side was the surgeon. 'Are you okay?' he was asked by his mother. He nodded, and then turned to a nurse and asked 'Can I have my tonsils now?'

The nurse explained that the tonsils had already been thrown away. 'No you didn't,' replied Ingo. 'You put them behind those over there. Give them to me.' He then looked back at his mother. 'Mama,' he said, 'the doctor said a naughty word when he cut my tongue.'

Both his mother and the nurse were surprised, not only at the request but also the fact that young Ingo knew exactly where the glass bottle containing the tonsils was located, particularly as the bottle and its bloody contents were hidden behind the two rolls of tissue.[27]

It seems that, with the exception of one or two ideas, that he had experienced earlier incarnations, Ingo's early years were uneventful. He had an army career and then he moved to New York to work at the United Nations for 11 years.

In 1969 he resigned from the UN and decided to follow his creative urges and become a painter. At this time he also decided to add a second 'n' to his surname. He was not particularly successful as a painter and, after a series of incidents with his pet chinchilla in which the animal seemed to pick up his thoughts, Swann became involved in psychical research, eventually working in the New York laboratories of a researcher called Cleve Backster. He was keen to assist in the experiments and in 1971 he was involved in a series of tests to isolate psychic abilities at the American Society for Psychical Research. He was ready and willing to have this skill tested and volunteered to undertake a series of tests. How he gained the reputation for being able to project his astral body to other locations is not entirely clear, but by the end of the year he had been the subject of a series of experiments designed by Dr Karlis Otis and his assistant, Janet Mitchell.

These experiments involved Swann sitting in a chair and projecting himself out of his body to observe objects that had been set out of sight on a platform suspended from the ceiling. The experimenters left the room leaving Swann unobserved. The argument was used that Swann could not have taken any sneak peeks because his head had a series of electrodes attached and any movement would have been recorded. He was supplied with a clipboard and a pen, which he used for making sketches of what he perceived. Critics have pointed out that, although his outstretched hand may not have been able to reach the platform, he could have simply raised his hand and used a mirror to look at the contents of the shelf. I simply cannot understand why it was felt necessary to leave Swann unobserved during the crucial parts of the experiment. Surely the designers of the experiment would have known that such a thing would invite questioning of what is an exceptional series of results.

The magician Milbourne Christopher has asked an even simpler question – why was it necessary to have the objects in the same room as the subject? To this he has added, why were the objects placed so close to Swann?

That Swann may have used a mirror to look at the objects is reinforced by the fact that he was aware of all the objects, but missed the four numbers that were written on something located to the side, in exactly the position that would have not been visible if a reflecting surface had been angled near the end.

Whatever took place in that enclosed room, the results were astonishing. As regards the objects, he correctly identified all eight. Otis calculated that the odds of these being lucky guesses were greater than 40,000 to 1. It is clear that Swann did seem to have the ability to perceive things that were not available through normal perceptions. What was needed was further empirical work into this amazing skill.

The Mind-Reach Years

A few months later, the opportunity arose. In early 1972 Ingo had popped in to see his old friend Cleve Backster. Backster's laboratories had continued to measure successfully the electrical activities of plants using standard lie-detector equipment. This work had come to the attention of Dr Harold Puthoff of Stanford University in California. Puthoff was keen to do some basic research into what he termed 'quantum biology' and he was sure that the results of Backster's experiments had implications for his own research. Puthoff had written to Backster and this letter was spotted by Swann. Puthoff's proposal was of great interest to Swann, so he decided to send a letter back to California explaining what skills he had shown during earlier experiments and how these skills could be of use to Puthoff.

Eventually Puthoff gained funding from Science Unlimited Research of San Antonio in Texas, and on the strength of Swann's letter, he decided to invite Ingo to his laboratory at Stanford

University in California. Puthoff planned to spend a week testing out Swann's abilities and to see if they could be used as a vehicle for the testing of biological effects in light of quantum mechanics.

On 6 June 1972 Puthoff met Swann at San Francisco airport. Not wishing to waste any time, Puthoff informed Swann that they would be going straight to Stanford's Varian Physics Building to meet up with Dr Arthur Hebbard. In the vault of this building was an apparatus called a magnetometer, consisting of a magnetic probe used to measure small oscillations in the magnetic field surrounding the apparatus. It was believed that any fluctuations in this field might suggest the presence of quarks – mysterious elementary particles thought to be found within protons, at that time the smallest 'bit' of matter that had been discovered.

As the magnetometer needed to be well shielded from the environment, it had been placed five feet below the floor of the building in a purpose-built vault. Surrounding the magnetic probe was an aluminium container, copper shielding, and even a superconducting shield that was the best available at the time.

The magnetometer had been running for about an hour before Puthoff and Swann had arrived and a stable pattern of oscillations had been traced on the chart recorder. Puthoff then asked Swann if he could affect the device in any way.

Swann obliged by focusing his attention on the interior of the vault. Initially he 'saw' nothing, but then something very strange happened. The oscillation level, as recorded by the magnetometer, suddenly doubled and continued at this rate for about 30 seconds. Swann then claimed that he couldn't hold his attention any longer and the oscillations returned to normal.

The researchers were intrigued. When asked how he had affected the probe, Swann explained that in his mind's eye he had a direct vision of the apparatus. He then sketched what he 'saw'. He surprised

Puthoff by commenting upon a gold alloy plate within the interior. This was indeed correct and Puthoff was sure that there was no way that Swann could know this.

As a quantum physicist Puthoff was aware that one version of quantum theory suggests that the act of observation can have a direct effect upon the behaviour of subatomic particles. I will discuss this in greater detail later in the book, but for the moment it is important to be aware that observation is a crucial element within particle physics. Puthoff was intrigued by the possibility that Swann had, in some way, actually 'observed' the electromagnetic field and affected it in some way. Of course, this implied that he had an ability to 'see' things that he could not possibly see by using vision alone.

However, the following day Hebbard reported that the magnetometer was malfunctioning. It has been suggested that problems with the machine were such that the researchers decided not to repeat the experiment. The question is, was the malfunctioning of the magnetometer caused by the 'observation' of Swann or did the malfunctioning cause the 'blip' in the oscillations of the magnetic field surrounding the probe?

It is clear from subsequent enquiries taken up by writer Scott Rogo that Dr Hebbard was as intrigued by these results as was Puthoff. As soon as Swann had felt he could not concentrate any longer, the doubling of the oscillation ceased and the rate immediately returned to normal. This has to be of significance and does suggest that in some way Ingo's observation affected the magnetometer.

The fascinated Puthoff quickly set up a series of fairly simple but effective experiments to test Swann's skills. An object would be placed in a thick-walled wooden case. This would then be locked. Swann would then be brought into the room and asked to describe what was in the box. In his book *Mind Reach* Puthoff states that he was delighted with the results. Unfortunately, he does not give any data, so we have no idea if Swann described the contents of the box correctly every time, 75 per cent of the time or 10 per cent of the time. However, he does state that he was so pleased he invited the financial sponsors to witness Swann's abilities for themselves. He cites one particular example in which a live moth had been captured and placed in the box. In front of witnesses Ingo described the contents of the box as being:

> something small, brown and irregular, sort of like a
> leaf, or something that resembles it but it is very much
> alive, like it's even moving![28]

This was a very impressive 'hit' and it tells much about the nature of remote viewing. The information is not clear and the perceiver has to make sense of confusing images. If Swann could clearly see the contents of the box then he would have immediately realized that it was a moth and identified it as such.

These examples of mental bi-location impressed Puthoff sufficiently for him to invite Swann to be involved in an intensive eight-month study of his abilities. By this stage Dr Puthoff had been joined in his research by Russell Targ, a specialist in lasers and plasma research and a renowned researcher into parapsychological phenomena. Indeed, he had just completed a six-week investigation of Uri Geller before joining Puthoff at the Stanford Research Institute (SRI).

Working With Coordinates

A few months later Swann returned to Stanford to start the intensive set of experiments that Targ and Puthoff had devised for him. Over a period of weeks the results were considered to be of 'statistical significance', but nothing really outstanding had been observed.

This clearly concerned Swann and he was keen to impress the research team with his skills. Obviously he wanted the tests to be designed with his having a greater degree of control over methods and process. One day, he suggested that a more challenging test of his remote viewing skills would be for the researchers to give him a set of geographical coordinates for anywhere on the planet and he would describe what he 'saw' when he projected himself to that location. Initially Puthoff and Targ were not sure about this suggestion. In the book *Mind-Reach*, Puthoff suggests this was because he and his associate thought it would be very difficult both to set up the experiment and for Swann to be successful.

I find this rather strange. Geographical coordinates are man-made constructs. If Swann intended to astrally travel to a suggested location how would he know that he was in the correct place? There are no external cues by which he could navigate himself to the precise spot. However, a good visual memory and knowledge of geography could really assist in this regard. I am in the fortunate position of having both these skills. I tested myself by looking at an atlas with longitude and latitude lines and then memorizing what I saw. As the lines in both directions follow a basic numeric sequence, one only needs to memorize a handful of crucial coordinates (0 degrees latitude is the Equator, 20 degrees north goes close to Mexico City and Mumbai, 20 degrees south goes close to Belo Horizonte in Brazil and Bulawayo in Zimbabwe, and so forth). It is fair to conclude that Swann, as an American, would also know that the border between the USA and Canada follows the 50th parallel. Regarding longitude, a similar set of visual coordinates can be memorized (0 degrees is Greenwich, 100 degrees west goes near Mexico City, 100 degrees east near Bangkok). Knowing the mileage between each degree also assists in quickly visualizing a location. More significantly, what Swann was suggesting here is virtually identical to the 'weather' remote-viewing experiments that Swann had been involved with when being tested by Janet Mitchell the previous year. Clearly this was something he knew himself to be good at. In his own writing he happily points out that he was an extremely precocious and gifted child, one who at the tender age of three years had read a dictionary from cover to cover and between the ages of four and seven had read the *entire Encyclopaedia Britannica*. Memorizing a series of coordinates to identify locations on a map would be, literally, 'child's play'.

Targ and Puthoff agreed. Swann was given a series of coordinates and asked to report what he saw. This is how it is described in *Mind-Reach*:

> 'Seventy-five degrees north, forty-five degrees west.'
> 'Ice.' 'Fifteen degrees north, one hundred twenty
> degrees east.' 'Land, jungles, mountains, peninsular
> mountains.' 'Thirty-eight degrees north, twenty-nine
> degrees west.' 'In my immediate vicinity, ocean. I see
> Spain off in the distance. And so it went on. Not bad,
> not bad.'[29]

Seventy-five degrees north is very far north – Baffin Island, mid-Greenland and Spitsbergen. Swann, not surprisingly, reports 'Ice'. The second coordinate, 15 degrees north, 120 east, is clearly just north of the equator and as such it is highly probable that it will be jungle wherever it is along the line of longitude. But he hedges his bets with a list of mountains and peninsular mountains; logical really, as the location, for anybody with basic geographical knowledge, is likely to be Indonesia, which has mountains and peninsulas surrounded by sea. In many ways this highlights why this process leaves a genuine 'distance viewer' open to reasonable attack from sceptics.

However, the final statement contains genuine mystery. By my calculation 29 degrees west is in the Atlantic Ocean at that latitude.

Swann correctly identifies the area around him as sea – he can see 'Spain off in the distance'. For me this is real remote viewing, as the nearest land is 38.6 miles away and that land is not Spain but Ilha do Faial in the Azores, belonging to Portugal. I am also sure, at that distance Ilha do Faial would clearly have been seen as an island.

But what mystifies me even more is how he knows (incorrectly) that this 'land' is Spain? How can anybody identify a landmass over 35 miles away as being part of a particular country? This does rather suggest that he was visualizing a map of the world in his mind and incorrectly assumed that he would be able to see 'Spain'.

Clearly the error in identifying a Portuguese island as the Spanish mainland was simply that, in general, the scenery to be found in Portugal is very similar to that of its Spanish neighbour. From a distance of more than 30 miles this is more an error of identification than proof that Swann was pretending to see the target and using a basic knowledge of geography.

In all, Swann was given 100 locations to identify spread over 10 groups of 10. In *Mind Reach* Puthoff and Targ present a chart showing the results of the last group. The experimenters consider these to be good examples of the 'surprising precision that sometimes occurred'. Of the 10, Puthoff and Targ consider 7 to be 'hits', 2 to be neutral and 1 to be a 'miss'. In my personal opinion the allocation of a 'hit' to some of these was somewhat generous. For 42 degrees north, 105 degrees east, Swann uses a single word description, 'mountains' and for 45 degrees north, 150 west, we get 'ocean' with a nice description of what colour waves are. Indeed, for 30 degrees south and zero degrees we have another colourful description of waves (deep blue). Not one of the descriptions are specific in any way and, as I have stated earlier, for somebody of Swann's self-stated intellectual abilities, such educated guesses are not that hard to come by.

Intrigued by these results, Puthoff and Targ set up a pilot study in spring 1973. Members of their research team supplied a series of targets and they also received suggested locations from interested scientists in other laboratories. They were keen to see whether Ingo was using eidetic memory to describe the locations. Eidetic memory is more popularly known as 'photographic memory'. This is an ability that certain individuals have to hold an image in their 'mind's eye' of something they have seen previously. There was a possibility that Swann had this ability and had 'memorized' a map of the world with the coordinates shown. All he had to do when given a latitude and longitude coordinate was visualize the map and read off the coordinates to find the location. Only a reasonable knowledge of geography was then needed. To ensure that this was not the case they set up a protocol they called *Project Scanate*. Scanate was a portmanteau word made up from *scan*ning by coordin*ate*. Scanate demanded that the subject supply detail beyond that available simply from looking at a map. For example, Ingo would be required to describe the buildings and other man-made structures located at the supplied coordinate.

The first test involved Ingo identifying a location on the French South Indian Ocean island of Kerguelen. This was quite successful in that he not only identified the geographical features, but also a set of buildings with a radio antenna and two white, cylindrical tanks. He added that to the northwest was a small airstrip, and two or three trucks were parked outside the building.

That he identified a windswept sub-Antarctic island is not as impressive. By simple memory, eidetic or otherwise, he would know the rough location and therefore the rather general description of the 'rocky' terrain could describe most places at that latitude. Of course, the coordinates could have been open ocean, but as this test was to describe man-made buildings, it was fairly reasonable to conclude that it would be a landmass. That far south in the Indian and Pacific oceans are only a handful of island groups: Prince Edward Island, Crozet Island, McDonald Island, Heard Island and Kerguelen. All these have very similar geography. Not at all surprisingly each one has a research station manned by meteorologists and geologists. These people would need buildings to live in and communication systems with an 'antenna' and/or a satellite dish. They would also require storage tanks, trucks and an airstrip for supplies to be flown in. As such, is Ingo's description that convincing?

Ingo goes on to give some more specific descriptions of the coastline and then of boats and a jetty with snow-capped mountains, and states he sees one section that 'may be a lighthouse'. He also drew a map of the island that is similar to Kerguelen. Targ and Puthoff were impressed by this and point out that Kerguelen had, at that time, a Soviet-French research facility.

I have done my own research into Kerguelen. Now I have no information of what was on the island in 1972, but as of 2010 the islands have no airport of any description. However, there are two lighthouses at the entrance to the harbour at Port au Francais. These are quite close to each other and therefore would have been 'seen' as part of the same vista.

The next test was to prove a stunning success. This time the coordinates were given by an external team, keen to challenge the results of the SRI experiments. The coordinates were given and Ingo had to give an immediate response. It was a target site somewhere on the east coast of the USA. This is how Ingo began his description:

> This seems to be some sort of mounds or rolling hills.
> There is a city to the north; I can see taller buildings
> and some smog. This seems to be a strange place,
> somewhat like the lawns that one would find around
> a military base, but I get the impression that there are

either some old bunkers around, or maybe a covered
reservoir. There must be a flagpole, some highways
to the west, possibly a river over to the far east, to the
south more city.[30]

Swann then sketched a detailed map of the area he perceived. He
drew a circular building, suggesting that it may have been a tower of
some sort. He added that there was something odd about the place,
insisting again that there was something underground.

Apparently, this was a fantastic hit. According to Puthoff and
Targ they received a phone call from the challenger a few weeks later,
confirming that everything was absolutely correct, even to the fact
that the relative distances on his drawing were accurate.

For those involved, these results were of such 'high quality' that
funding was found for a large-scale, three-year study of remote
viewing. This would take place at SRI under the control of Targ and
Puthoff. Subsequently, a series of double-blind tests took place with
local targets in the San Francisco Bay Area. With practice, Swann
became very proficient at identifying locations. For example, one
location was the Palo Alto City Hall. Ingo described a tall building
with 'set-in' windows. He then described a fountain but added that
'I cannot hear it'. Not only was his drawing of the location accurate,
but also he had correctly ascertained that the fountains outside
the building had been turned off. He also drew four trees at the
right of the building. This was again absolutely accurate. It was later
calculated that the chance of Ingo getting this right was in the order
of 2,500:1.

The project lasted 4 years with 55 separate experiments taking
place in that time. Many of these were successful. Indeed, such
was the confidence engendered by these results that the team
decided they were restricting themselves and should become more

ambitious. Having concluded that Ingo could 'view' at any distance they decided to test out just how far Ingo could 'distance view'.

Swann had long suggested that he could project himself far further than any locations on the planet Earth. He was keen to test this out. However, as Puthoff and Targ explained to him, any information he viewed could not be verified. Nonetheless, in April 1973 a unique opportunity presented itself.

The Mission to Jupiter

At that time the NASA space probe *Pioneer 10* was approaching the planet Jupiter. If they moved quickly they could have Ingo supply information about the planet before the probe verified it. Ingo had already contacted another distance viewer by the name of Harold Sherman and the two of them had agreed to distance-view the giant planet. Sherman was based in Mountain View, Arkansas and had already developed a reputation as an effective and consistent viewer.

Initially, Puthoff and Targ had reservations about this exercise, but eventually agreed to record the experiment at SRI as a personal project rather than an official one.

On 27 April 1973 the group met at the lab and started the exercise at 6:00pm Pacific Standard Time. Simultaneously, Sherman similarly started his exercise in Mountain View. This was at 8:00pm Central Standard Time.

According to the transcript, at 6:03 Ingo reported that he was approaching a large, striped, planet. At 6:06 he was close enough to view the atmosphere. This is what he then described:

> Very high in the atmosphere there are crystals, they
> glitter. Maybe the stripes are like bands of crystals,
> maybe like rings of Saturn, though not far out like that.

> Very close within the atmosphere. I bet you they'll
> reflect radio probes. Is that possible if you had a cloud
> of crystals that were assaulted by different radio waves?[31]

What Ingo is describing here are rings around Jupiter. This was something unknown to astronomy at that time. Indeed, not even *Pioneer 10* was to confirm the existence of these structures. The following year another probe, *Pioneer 11,* suggested that such structures may exist, when measuring the planet's radiation belts, but it was to be another six years, in 1979, before *Voyager 1* confirmed their existence. This is, quite rightly, cited by many supporters of remote viewing as an irrefutable proof of Swann's abilities.

However, let us look at what Swann says in greater detail. He states that there are glittering bands of crystals, 'maybe like the rings of Saturn'. He then goes on to say that they are 'very close, within the atmosphere'. This is simply not how it is. According to the latest research the main ring (the one nearest the surface of the Jovian clouds) is 128,940 miles from the centre of the planet. It has a faint 'halo' that extends halfway to the surface, but even this halo ring is not, in any way 'within the atmosphere', by which I assume Swann means the clouds.

What has also been cited as significant is that both Sherman and Swann seemed to describe the same things at the same time. For example, Sherman describes what he can see:

> There appear to be huge volcanic peaks, great cones
> rising some miles.

And at the same time Ingo states:

> There is an enormous mountain range about thirty-one
> thousand feet high. Those mountains are huge.[32]

Here we have two individuals, 2,000 miles apart, seemingly sharing the same experience. This is, to me, of great significance as it is evidence of a consensual hallucination. I have used the word 'hallucination' because whatever Swann and Sherman were 'seeing' at that moment was not part of any astronomical reality that I am aware of. Why? Well, for one simple fact. Jupiter does not have any mountains. The latest research suggests that Jupiter may not even have any form of solid core. It is believed that the pressures and temperatures are so high that the hydrogen and helium that make up most of the Jovian atmosphere simply change from gas to liquid. As such, the 'surface' would be like an ocean of liquid helium and hydrogen. As on Earth, mountains cannot be made from a liquid. Even if Jupiter did have a solid core it is unlikely that this core would have anything remotely similar to what a human being would identify as a mountain. Furthermore, at that depth within the gas clouds of Jupiter, there would be very little, if any, natural light to see anything, let alone mountains. So in order to reach the solid core of the planet, Swann and Sherman would have had to fly through hundreds and hundreds of miles of dense gas to get to what little surface there may be. They do not describe any such journey. The furthest a probe has gone into the clouds of Jupiter is 130 miles (200km). This small machine was melted, crushed and vaporized on its journey in 1995. Indeed, the implication from their descriptions is that they viewed these mountains from a position out in space. Not only this, but their perceptions of these geological structures were amazingly precise. Sherman saw them as huge volcanic peaks and Ingo was sure that he even knew their height ('about 31,000 feet').

If these mountain ranges were visible from space and poking above the Jovian clouds then these 'mountains' would be considerably higher than 31,000 feet – more like 31,000 miles.

When he was later challenged on this point, Swann suggested that he may have seen another planet and confused it with Jupiter. This is not such an unreasonable suggestion. It will be recalled that his associate called the mountains 'volcanoes'. Some have criticized Swann for not noticing the moons, but I am of the opinion that he confused one of the moons for the surface of Jupiter. Io is the second closest satellite to the planet and does display a considerable variety of colours. It is clear that Swann had only a rudimentary knowledge of astronomy and therefore he would have carried certain assumptions as to what Jupiter would look like. The mainly reds, yellows and browns of the surface of this moon could easily look like Jupiter to the untrained eye.

However, it is significant to me that Io not only resembles its close neighbour, but also it has one other crucial geological feature that Jupiter does not have – volcanoes. It is even more significant that the existence of these features was only confirmed by *Voyager 1* in 1977. Even the potential existence of such mountains was suggested publicly just two weeks before the images were received.

If it was Io that Ingo saw during his remote viewing, then this is an incredible piece of evidence that he could, indeed, view remotely as he claimed.

A year later, in March 1974, Sherman and Swann repeated the experiment by focusing on the planet Mercury before the *Mariner 10* flyby. According to Swann, he and his associate recorded several pieces of data that were contrary to the predictions of the astronomers and subsequently proven by the *Mariner* flyby. These included the observation of a thin atmosphere, the existence of a small magnetic field and the existence of a helium trail in a direction leading away from the Sun.

I am absolutely convinced that Ingo Swann believes he actually perceives information by remote viewing. In his books and articles he comes across as a genuine and honest individual, but the evidence seems to contradict this. A close examination suggests that whatever he is seeing, it may not be what he thinks it is.

In my opinion he is remote viewing, but not doing so in this dimension. I believe that what Ingo, and all the other 'astral travellers' and distance viewers are doing is opening up their minds to a journey of a different nature; a journey to far-off places deep within the human psyche. They are all travelling in higher dimensions of reality that may look like this one, but are places of 'inner space'. In the last chapter Robert Monroe called this place Locale 3. In my opinion this is exactly where Swann, Sherman, Monroe and all the other distance viewers visit when they travel. They are not going out of the body at all. They are travelling inwards, travelling in 'inner space'.

I will present my case for this as this book progresses.

CHAPTER 6

The Modern Groups

The world wide web is full of organizations that offer training in astral travel and out-of-the-body experiences. For a fee, the initiate can be trained to view distant locations, visit friends and even travel into outer space. There is a huge industry built around this idea; it is clearly popular and I suspect this is because many people have experienced spontaneous ecsomatic experiences and wish to control them.

I have no doubt that these groups genuinely believe they can assist people in enjoying travels outside of the body. I also believe that the students do experience ecsomatic states during their training. The question for me is not whether the experiences are real, but whether the experience takes place in consensual reality or whether it is a far more exciting and mysterious altered state of consciousness. In this chapter I will review a small number of these groups.

The International Academy of Consciousness

One of the most interesting groups researching the out-of-body experience is the Brazilian-based organization the International Academy of Consciousness (IAC). The IAC was founded in 2000, but its roots go back to 1981 when Brazilian physician Dr Waldo Vieira founded the Centre for Continuous Consciousness (CCC) in Rio de Janeiro. For many years Vieira had undergone regular out-of-the-body experiences and he was keen to understand more about what was happening to him. In 1986 he published a book entitled *Projectiology – A Panorama of Experiences of the Consciousness Outside the Human Body*. Contained in its 1,232 pages is the most exhaustive review of the out-of-body experience ever compiled; the depth and range of this book is absolutely breathtaking. Its major purpose was to consolidate the ideas and theories of Dr Vieira and in doing so create a new science of consciousness that he calls Projectiology.

International interest in the ideas proposed in this work led to the creation in 1988 of the International Institute of Projectiology and Concientiology, which in turn developed into the IAC. In 1994 Vieira was to explain exactly what he meant by Concientiology in a further book entitled *700 Experiments of Concientiology*.

According to the literature of the IAC, Concientiology differs from conventional science in that its foundation is based upon a 'new, more advanced, philosophical paradigm'. Whereas our present Newtonian-Cartesian model only needs one level of reality (the physical universe), Concientiology suggests that there are many levels and that reality itself is not one-dimensional but multidimensional.

According to Concientiology we all have a psychic body as well as a physical body. This psychic body is termed the 'psychosoma' and this can leave the physical body, the soma, to travel both within this level of reality and also within the other many-layered dimensions that exist outside of our everyday awareness.

Concientiology goes on to agree with many religious groups that death is not the end and that consciousness itself evolves through various reincarnations. However, it also suggests that consciousness can continue to exist in a disembodied state and does not need a body in order to function effectively. Of course, this is in total contradiction to the present scientific belief that it is the brain that creates consciousness and at death consciousness simply ceases to exist.

In order to prove this philosophy the IAC have set up a purpose-built training campus near the town of Évoramonte, in the Alentejo region of Portugal. This facility also researches the nature of the out-of-body experience by applying another scientific concept that they call Projectiology. Projectiology is the systematic study of the ecsomatic state using a scientific method similar to that applied in university laboratories around the world. In doing so, it is hoped that the IAC will be able to present hard evidence that the psychosoma actually does leave the body and can perceive things not accessible to the soma.

Most of the Portuguese work takes place in two locations: in a building known as the Projectarium and another called the Waking Physical Immobility Laboratory, otherwise referred to as the Immobilitarium.

The Projectarium is a 29ft 6in-diameter spherical building that has been optimized for the facilitation of out-of-body states. The volunteer lies on a suspended platform with their head located at the centre of the spherical building. This gives the sensation of being in a void. It is clear from this description that the Projectarium is designed to evoke some form of sensory deprivation. As has been discovered in other similar experiments, the human mind, when deprived of external sensory stimuli, will start to create its own. In simple terms, the person will start to replace a seemingly nonexistent external reality with an internally created one.

The Immobilitarium evokes similar levels of sensory deprivation. In this case the subject is forced to remain immobile for three hours. This immobility includes the stopping of even swallowing or blinking. Again, IAC proudly states that such conditions regularly bring about self-reported out-of-body experiences.

Are these artificially created altered states of consciousness real or are they simply an hallucination? As we shall discover later in this book there are a handful of known psychological states in which sleep imagery can manifest itself into a waking mind that is deprived of sensory inputs. These can be very real, but actually are simply intrusions of sleep imagery into a wakeful mind. However interesting they may be, they are not evidence for genuine ecsomatic experiences.

IAC claims it has collected strong evidence that some subjects, whilst in these states, have been able to perceive information that would not have been available to their senses when inside the Immobilitarium and the Projectarium.

According to Dr Vieira and his fellow conscientiologists, travels outside the soma, are not dreams but real perceptions. He presents a series of reasons why he believes this to be the case. For example, he points out that in a dream there is no sensation of 'take-off'; dreamers simply find themselves in a dream location. In a projection, however, the projector perceives the leaving of the body and travelling through three-dimensional space to the final location. When in this location a projector takes an active role in what is taking place around them. This is not the case in a dream where the dreamer is simply a passive spectator. He further observes that in a projection the projector has increased awareness and the senses seem well developed, whereas in a dream everything appears slightly muffled and confusing.

I have never experienced a projection but, like most people, I do dream regularly, and my dreams are sometimes extremely vivid and they present to me a confused, and confusing, sensory experience. But in all my dreams I am not simply a spectator. I am fully involved in the narrative. People I encounter speak to me and I speak back to them. However, I have to admit that my dreams are never as powerfully sensory as those described by Vieira.

Having read Vieira's *Projections of the Consciousness – A Diary of Out-of-Body Experiences* I am struck by how similar his extra-soma locations are to those described by Monroe when he discusses Locale 2 and Locale 3. In the book, Vieira describes scores of projections and all of them involve him visiting a place, or places, that are totally divorced from the world of consensual experience – Monroe's Locale 1. He regularly encounters other projectors and entities that are clearly not of this plane of existence. He meets old friends and adversaries in situations extremely reminiscent of my own dreams. I have never considered these to be anything other than creations of my own subconscious. Occasionally he appears to stay in Locale 1 and, when he does, he takes the opportunity to 'visit' people he knows. Such a visit took place on 14 August 1979 when he projected himself to the state of Minas Gerais to find his sister. What is curious about his description of this event is that it seems to contradict his argument that there is a 'take-off' sensation and a feeling of travelling to the planned location. Here he describes how, at 3:35am, for his 'third sleep of the night' he 'lay down in the dorsal position, the ideal position for projections'. The next paragraph starts with 'I was completely awake as I respectfully entered the room of R., my sister and very close friend'.[33] This implies that one second he was in his bedroom in Ipanema, Rio de Janeiro, and the next in his sister's room in Minas Gerais, a few hundred miles north. Of course he may simply have omitted the journey itself, but a simple reading of his description implies that the journey from bedroom to bedroom was virtually instantaneous.

What then takes place is strongly reminiscent of Monroe's attempt to communicate with the laboratory technician at Charles Tart's facility and also Monroe's earlier failed telepathic communication with his friend, Dr Bradshaw. Vieira, by applying, as he terms it, 'mental force', manages to wake his sister. He then announces who he is. Not surprisingly his sister is disturbed by such a nocturnal visitation by a disembodied entity and asks him to leave her, accusing him of being a vampire. Worried by this reaction he leaves the room and walks round the house. He notices there is a light in the street outside that illuminated the room; then hearing a noise in another bedroom, he decides to leave the scene. Vieira then describes how his thoughts 'caused the psychosoma to levitate towards the ceiling'.

Again there is no description of a return journey to Rio. In the next paragraph he simply states: 'as I peacefully awoke, the projection felt as natural as any occurrence in human life.' Later that day he rang his sister who clearly recalled nothing of the incident. Indeed the only vaguely collaborative evidence for veridical perceptions on the part of Vieira was that there was another relative in the house and that his sister confirmed the existence of the external street lamp.

Now I cannot help but have questions regarding this incident. Vieira's psychosoma seemed to have no difficulty in finding not only his sister's home but also the correct bedroom. Of course, it could be that his soma had visited the house sometime in the past. But if this was the case, why did he make such a play of the fact that he was able to identify that a streetlight illuminated the living room, when surely he would have known this to be the case from a previous visit?

More importantly, in exactly the same way as the laboratory

technician and Dr Bradshaw did not recall any communication, telepathic or otherwise, with Robert Monroe's astral body, so it was with Waldo Vieira's sister. She remembered nothing of the incident, even though it was seemingly quite disturbing for her as far as Vieira was concerned.

Is this yet again evidence that wherever individuals such as Waldo Vieira, Robert Monroe, Ingo Swann and George Ritchie found themselves when out of body, it is certainly not Locale 1?

Hemi-Sync®

As we have discovered, Robert Monroe experienced a series of fascinating altered states of consciousness. These states seemed to give his consciousness an awareness of alternative realities. He called these realities 'Locales' and suggested that there were at least three.

It was never fully explained why Robert was able to travel outside of his body, but clearly it had something to do with his brain or, more specifically, the way in which his brain processed external information received through the senses. He described how many of his ecsomatic adventures started with a vibration that built up within his head and enveloped his whole body. Observing this many times, he became convinced that his body oscillated at 4Hz – hertz is the standard measurement of frequency and it quantifies the number of cycles per second of any periodic phenomenon. In this case we are describing brain waves. This suspicion was subsequently confirmed by a group of research scientists who joined Robert at his home, Whistlefield, in the early 1970s. These included electrical engineer Dennis Mennerich, audio engineer Bill Yost and physicist Tom Campbell.

Mennerich and Campbell suspected there was a specific part of the brain that was responsible – a small structure that sits deep within the brain, nestled between the two hemispheres – the pineal gland. As we have already discovered, this mysterious organ was, and still is, central to many mystic traditions including the Bön of Tibet and the Theosophists. This may simply be because it is the only organ within the brain that is not part of a pair. Every other structure found within one hemisphere of the brain is mirror-imaged in another identical organ in the other hemisphere. This had been noted since ancient times and our ancestors were fascinated as to why this small, pea-sized object resembling a pine cone (hence its name) was not part of a pair of organs. This had to be of significance; but how?

The French philosopher René Descartes was convinced that this mysterious organ was the location of the soul. His logic was powerful. Descartes suggested that we had two eyes and two ears supplying the respective hemispheres with information. This information was then reduced down and supplied to one central point within the brain, and that place, where it all came together, was the pineal gland. This reflected the more esoteric beliefs that this tiny object was the 'third eye', the window through which consciousness can 'see' the other worlds denied to the external organs of sight which, by looking out rather than in, can only perceive the external, material world.

As we have seen, later esoteric traditions such as the Theosophists argued that the pineal gland is some form of 'stargate' that can open up human awareness to enlightenment. To others it is the sixth chakra whose awakening is linked to prophesy and increased psychic awareness. Indeed, it was in her book *The Secret Doctrine*, published in 1888, that the founder of Theosophy, Helena Blavatsky, reintroduced to Western occultism the importance of this curious organ.

However, it was a 1929 book entitled *The Projection of the Astral Body* that was to stimulate Mennerich and Campbell's interest in the role of the pineal gland in the out-of-body experience. In this book the authors, psychic researcher Hereward Carrington and astral traveller Sylvan Muldoon suggested that this organ was, in some way, directly responsible for the phenomenon.

In his own fascinating book, *My Big Toe – Awakening*, Tom Campbell describes in detail how he and his associates took the suggestions of Carrington and Muldoon and applied them to modern scientific and engineering principles. They designed a huge capacitor that would generate a uniform and strong electric field. This capacitor fed two 2ft-square plates with a charge of 250,000 volts, which in turn generated a 4Hz AC signal. With the capacitor working at full power, Tom placed his head between the plates and tried to reach an altered state. After an hour he started to feel distinctly odd and his head began, as he describes it, to 'wobble dangerously between the two plates'.[34] They then experimented with various other processes, but it was an article in the October 1973 edition of *Scientific American* that was to give the researchers the breakthrough they needed.

It was a short article by Gerald Oster entitled 'Auditory Beats in the Brain'. Oster was describing a phenomenon known as *binaural beats*. What Oster had observed was that if a pure tone of, for example, 100Hz was played in one ear of a subject and a similar tone of 104Hz in the other ear, then the subject will perceive not only the 100 and 104Hz frequencies, but also a third frequency of 4Hz. Mennerich read this article with increasing excitement, as this process presented a potential solution to the problem of how to isolate a 4Hz oscillation and administer it directly to the brain.

Mennerich then created an audiotape that reproduced the sounds suggested by Oster and, after testing, it was found to have powerful effects on states of consciousness. Indeed, they discovered that they could reproduce the experiences that Robert Monroe had been encountering naturally for many years, and in doing so they could offer everybody a return ticket to the place Monroe called 'Non-Physical Matter Reality' or NPMR.

In a series of amazing experiments, Campbell and the team were able to bring about remote-viewing states, manifesting lights in the sky, visiting distant locations, and travels into Monroe's Locales 2 and 3.

Such was the power of this process that Dennis Mennerich and Tom Campbell volunteered for a series of tests to measure the effectiveness of remote viewing. In his book Tom claims that they correctly identified every target they were given. Not only that, but during these tests they had been attached to an EEG machine to measure their brain activity whilst in these ecsomatic states. It seems that when the EEG scrolls were returned to Duke University, Dennis had produced the highest level of alpha waves ever recorded at the university.

Why this process is so effective can be explained by a phenomenon known as *synchrony*. When the two aural signals encounter each other in the centre of the brain they produce synchronized, coherent electromagnetic energy within the brain. This energy is similar to a laser beam and, as we shall see later in this book, this is of astounding significance when discussed in relation to some exciting new developments in neurology and neurochemistry.

This process was patented by the Monroe Institute and is known as the 'Hemi-Sync®'. Many amazing claims are now made with regard to the procedure and I am unsure whether these are approved by the Institute or not. For example, it is said that this device can facilitate the following abilities: you can illuminate light bulbs with your own energy, bend spoons with minimal effort, accelerate healthy plant growth and influence computers, dice and slot machines! It can also accelerate the 'law of attraction'. However, what is no longer mentioned is the reason for which it was first developed.

Tom Campbell continued with his work in this area and he has now developed a fascinating concept called 'My Big Toe'. This is a real 'theory of everything' and it is to this we now turn our attention.

Tom Campbell's Big Toe

For Tom Campbell, each one of us has our own personal big-TOE. TOE is an acronym for 'Theory of Everything' and what he is suggesting is that we filter external information depending upon our own life experiences and education. Therefore, what we perceive as 'reality' is, in fact, a reality limited by our fears, beliefs and all the other things that build up our image of the way the world works.

This filter is so effective that it restricts our perceptions of the many levels of reality that actually exist. He uses an analogy of a bacterium in the small intestine with a very restricted understanding of what reality really consists of. If we were bacteria we would have no understanding of such things as trees, mountains or sunsets. All that can be understood by this life form is only defined by what it has experienced deep within the gut.

There is a much-cited story, no doubt apocryphal, that the original inhabitants of Central America on first encountering the ships of the Spanish Conquistadors simply did not see them. Such things were outside of their big-TOE and, as such, simply did not exist. Whether this story is true or not is beside the point. What it does do is present an excellent example of what Campbell is trying to explain.

The physical reality that is presented to each consciousness, through the big-TOE filter mechanism, Campbell terms physical matter reality or PMR. However, there is a much broader reality that is excluded from each PMR. He terms this, not unsurprisingly, non-physical matter reality or NPMR.

This suggests the reality that you and I perceive through our senses is an internally created illusion fabricated from memories, education, the mass media and many other factors. If this is the case, then why do other consciousnesses seem to share this illusion? Why is objective reality the same for everybody?

Tom Campbell has an answer. He points out that we all have the same physiology, so all our sense organs pick up the same inputs. To this is added another factor – we all share similar cultural norms. Therefore, it is not surprising that we all see the world in roughly the same way. In support of this position it has long been known by sociologists and linguists that language itself can manipulate how people build models of the external world. A particularly interesting theory by Edward Sapir and Benjamin Lee Whorf proposes that grammar can model perception in the most profound ways. It was noted that the Hopi language of the Native Americans in the southwest does not treat the flow of time as a sequence of distinct countable elements as do all European languages. In the Hopi language time is a single, continual process. For example, the concept of 'the next bus will arrive in two hours' cannot be translated into Hopi and therefore has no meaning. This suggested to Whorf that for the Hopi speaker, duration is a quite alien concept, whereas for a European such a concept rules how things work. I can verify this since I visited a Hopi reservation in northern Arizona, in the summer of 2009, and was told by an English speaker that he was amazed at the patience of the local Hopi people – they never get upset when delays take place at their local 'fast-food' outlet, whereas all non-Hopi speakers quickly get frustrated and vocal if they have to wait longer than anticipated.

So we all share, to a certain extent, our PMR but add our own idiosyncrasies. Is this why people argue and fall out over seemingly trivial things? Are they failing to communicate because they are genuinely seeing things differently? This certainly would explain clashes of cultures or of religious groups. Extrapolating further, this suggests that people who strongly believe in things such as the efficacy of prayer and the existence of UFOs, may model their PMR to accommodate such beliefs and in doing so reinforce those beliefs both individually and collectively.

Because PMR is such a beguiling and seemingly consistent reality, most people when they encounter NPMR simply cannot process it in any rational or structured way. The only tools available are metaphors and symbols supplied from PMR. These have specific meanings for each perceiving consciousness; meanings that indeed may be very different from person to person.

We encounter NPMR when we dream or we move into altered states of consciousness such as that of an ecsomatic experience. However, whilst in these states, we carry with us our internal model of what reality should be. We assume that we are still 'located' somewhere in space-time and that we 'see' and 'hear' things through our senses.

For Campbell this explains why during certain out-of-body experiences, such as a near-death experience, the person seems to encounter a world very similar to our own. The classic NDE involves meetings with dead relatives and religious icons such as Jesus, the Virgin Mary or the Hindu god of death. Clearly the cultural bias of each experience suggests that there is an underlying substance to these experiences that is not perceived. The PMR model carries through into NPMR and is used to make sense of something entirely alien.

Campbell's model of NPMR is strongly reminiscent of the shamanic world described to me by Gary Plunkett and Sebastian Cheatham. The upper and lower worlds are inhabited by all kinds of archetypes that seem to manifest from the deep subconscious of the experiencer. These symbolic beings appear to be as much related to Jung's collective unconscious as to the deep memories of the dreamer. It is as if the ecsomatic world is created by the mind for the mind.

However, Campbell is of the opinion that we are wrong to assume that neurochemistry of any description is involved in the ecsomatic experience. In a personal communication he gave me an interesting analogy. He wrote:

> Saying that neurological mechanisms are the cause (or enabler) of accessing Locale 2, is like saying that seeds cannot germinate without farmers – of course there is a relationship, most seeds do germinate because of farmers – but it is faulty logic to then come to the conclusion that seeds would be unable to generate if farmers did not exist.

But what about consensual reality – the place that we share with others? According to Campbell that, too, is not quite what it seems. He believes that what we perceive as reality is a huge simulation he calls physical matter reality or PMR. We perceive the PMR as we perceive a first-person computer game, such as the hugely popular *Second Life*. What we interact with through our senses is actually a form of hologram projected into our consciousness by something that Campbell calls 'The Big Computer' (TBC). What we 'see', 'hear' and 'feel' is rendered by the program as we attend to things around us. Until objects are brought into existence by an act of observation they only exist in potential. This is very similar to something we will encounter later called the Copenhagen Interpretation of quantum physics.

Tom Campbell's *My Big Toe* model is tremendously powerful as an explanation of subjective experience. I have discussed his model in some detail with him and I strongly believe that this concept presents a viable new way in which ecsomatic experiences can be explained whilst still using elements of our modern scientific paradigm.

I was keen to know if Tom's strongly scientific model is reflected in any spiritual path or religious teaching. Much to my surprise and delight I found an organization that, although seemingly oblivious to My Big Toe, certainly seems to be exploring similar pathways of the mind. This is the strangely named Eckankar organization. It is to this fascinating new religion that we now turn our attention.

Eckankar and Soul Travelling

According to the information available from its website, Eckankar's teachings have very ancient roots. These were rediscovered by a Kentuckian by the name of Paul Twitchell. At the age of three, Twitchell was taught the art of what he termed 'soul travel' from his elder sister. Twitchell explains in his books that this knowledge had been given to her by their father, who in turn had been taught the technique by an Indian guru called Sudar Singh.

Soul travelling, now a central tenant of the Eckankar spiritual path, is clearly a form of lucid dreaming or astral travel in which the subject travels into other planes of existence and in doing so can develop their own inner godliness.

In 1944, at the age of 35, Twitchell was soul-travelling when he encountered a Tibetan master by the name of Rebazar Tarzs. The master explained that he had travelled in his 'soul body' from his earthly location near to the Katsupari monastery in northern Tibet in order to impart to Twitchell something called ECK – the power or Spirit of God.

This sent Twitchell on a spiritual quest that saw his involvement with many of the 'new religions', including a group known as the Ruhani Satsang and another, much more famous religion, called

Scientology. This was all part of the training he needed to inherit the mantle of a living ECK master and, in 1965, he announced to the world that he was number 971 in an unbroken line that stretched back many thousands of years. In 1970 he established Eckankar as a non-profit religious organization. When he died in 1971, he left a growing and financially stable organization to Living Master number 972, Darwin Gross. The Church's headquarters then moved to California. At the present time the Church's senior member is Living Master number 973, Harold Klemp, and its headquarters have now relocated to Chanhassen, near Minneapolis.

Critics have pointed out that much of the teaching of Eckankar has been taken from another group known as the Sant Mat (the Path of Saints). Now this is fascinating because Sant Mat teaches that everything lies within us and that God is within. Their practices involve listening to the 'inner sound' and the 'inner light' and eventually leaving the body at will. This is termed 'dying while living' and involves unification with God within by the waking of the soul. To do this, the adherents have to connect to something within called the *surat* – this is the soul, or 'attention'. They sit with eyes closed and focus their attention on the pineal gland while repeating one or more mantras. This is called *simran* or repetition. It is fascinating that modern Sant Mat teaching involves perceiving something called the *shabd* or *sound current*. This can only be heard after initiation and a deliberate focus on the pineal gland. The *shabd* then becomes the source of inner light. It is known that in the early 1960s Paul Twitchell was an initiate of Sant Kirpal Singh, a practitioner of *Surat Shabd Yoga*.

There are intriguing similarities between Surat Shabd Yoga and the teachings of Eckankar. As we know, *shabd* means 'sound' or 'word' and *surat* means 'attention' in Arabic. *Yoga* means 'union'. In this context 'word' (*shabd*) means the 'sound current' or the 'audible life stream' that was sent out as a sound vibration by the Supreme Being into the abyss of space at the dawn of the universe. So Surat Shabd Yoga is the union of the soul with the essence of the Absolute Supreme Being.

As with Kabbalah and Theosophy, Surat Shabd Yoga teaches that there are eight spiritual levels existing above the spiritual plane. Self-realization is attained at the third level, called *Daswan Dwar,* Spirit realization at the fourth level, *Bhanwar Gupha* and God realization at the fifth level, *Sat Lok.*

But let us now return to the teachings of Eckankar. As we have already discovered, Eckankar teaches that the soul (the true self) can leave the body and travel within other planes of reality. This is called 'soul travel' and in order to 'soul-travel' a practitioner needs to shift their awareness from the body to the inner planes of existence. This seems rather a contradiction, unless soul travel is, as described, an inner journey within inner space. In order to block out the sensations given to the mind by the senses ECKists sing or chant the word 'hu' (pronounced 'hue').

According to Eckankar there are 11 worlds of existence. These consist of 5 'lower worlds' (psychic or material) and 6 upper (spiritual) planes. Each has a regular name, a classical name and an associated sound and light. The lower planes are:

- the physical plane (the material world)
- the astral plane
- the causal plane (where memories of previous lives are stored – the Akashic Record maybe?)
- the mental plane which contains the sources of ethics and moral teaching
- the etheric plane that is the boundary with the 'upper worlds'.

Interestingly, Eckankar teaches that the astral plane is the 'source of human emotion, psychic phenomena, ghosts and UFOs'. This sounds very like Monroe's Locale 2.

ECKists describe how, by soul travel, the individual moves closer to what they term the 'Heart of God'. Intriguingly, they seem to agree with Tom Campbell when they say that space and time do not exist in the higher planes, but the illusion of fast travel is conveyed so that the soul may comprehend in its own way that it is travelling. When soul travel starts, the experiencer will hear a 'rushing sound, like a wailing wind in a tunnel, along with a sensation of incredible speed'. This is very similar to the reports of NDEs.

The process of soul travel, as described on their website, makes fascinating reading when applying some of the ideas suggested in this book. Central to the process is the activation of what ECKists call the '*Tisra Til*'. It comes as no surprise that this is the 'Third Eye' or pineal gland. The website explains that this is 'a place where soul – you, as a conscious, individual spark of God – resides'.

The soul traveller then starts singing the word 'hu'. The experiencer on the website claims that he then found himself spirited to his home in Minneapolis and to the couch in his living room. He then perceives his children playing and notes that his wife, April, was busying herself in the kitchen. Significantly, he states that 'although it all seemed just my imagination, it still felt real.' In other words he was somewhere else, but not in this version of reality. Note that he does not describe any form of journey to his home. He simply finds himself there. There is no transition. This is exactly what would be expected if, in fact, this was a lucid-dream state. Similarly, when he is 'called back' by the facilitators he does not describe any journey, simply that he is back in his body in the training room in Los Angeles. It is interesting that, on his return home, his wife confirmed that one of the children stated that he saw the father standing in the kitchen with his hand on his wife's shoulder. This was at exactly the same time that the astral traveller had had his ecsomatic experience but, curiously, the experiencer did not describe standing next to his wife or putting his hand on her shoulder. Clearly, there is some level of confusion as to what exactly took place.

The organization is quite precise in that its soul travel is much more than simply a version of astral travel. As the website states:

> Dreams and visions are a fascinating subject. Yet an ECKist finds that Soul Travel probes a lot deeper into the riddle of life than do any astral or mental projections. Hence his goal is total awareness, and he puts away the toys of psychic phenomena ...[35]

For ECKists, dreams are considered to be of utmost importance; they are advised to keep extensive dream journals. Totally in keeping with my model, they believe that effective dream travel will serve as a gateway to soul travel. Could this not be interpreted as non-lucid dreaming changing into lucid dreaming after training? By doing this a practitioner can move their consciousness into ever higher states of being. One of the major teaching books of the movement is called *The Art of Spiritual Dreaming*. This gives many techniques that are similar to those found in books on lucid dreaming. Yet again it is clear that what Eckankar is really teaching is travel within the inner planes of our inner space.

In strong echoes of Surat Shabd Yoga, Eckankar teaches that by travelling through the spiritual levels the soul can become initially self-realized and ultimately achieve 'God realization'. Indeed, the membership card given to all Eckankar members states:

> The aim and purpose of Eckankar has always been to take soul by its path back to its divine source.

This has echoes of the Gnostic teaching of the Persian mystic, Mani, and has many parallels with the Gnostic idea that we all have an element of ourselves that is part of the 'light' of the Pleroma – the reality behind the illusory created by the Demiurge.

So here we have a fascinating melange of teachings, most of which are taken from much more ancient traditions. Again it is clear that these beliefs are rooted in an acceptance that soul travel is an inner, not outer, journey, in which the subject exists in a universe created by the mind but greater than the mind.

It still begs questions regarding the ultimate nature of these experiences. Are they actually *real* or just some form of dream that seems somehow more real than a dream; a dream that can be inhabited and manipulated?

Surprisingly, many individuals from all around the world have reported this in-between state exactly. It is called lucid dreaming and it is to this intriguing altered state of consciousness that we now turn our attention.

CHAPTER 7

The Mystery of Lucid Dreaming

False Awakenings

In 1976 researcher Stewart Twemlow wrote an article for a US national magazine in which he asked for responses from any readers who had experienced an out-of-body state. The results of this survey were eventually published in the *American Journal of Psychiatry* in April 1982.[36] Of the 1,500 responses, 700 reported experiences that involved the perception of total separation of mind and body.

In 1977, two follow-up questionnaires were sent out to all 700 in the subset. These were the POBE (Profile of Out-of-Body Experiences) and the PAL (Profile for the Adaptation to Life). The researchers received 339 responses in which both questionnaires were completed. The results are of great interest as they show that individuals who report OBEs are normal and show no real psychological extremes. However, there were two results of this survey that I consider to be of great significance. Firstly, in the Twemlow survey only 58 per cent reported that the out-of-body (OOB) environment was the same as that where their body was located. By extrapolation this tells us that 142 reported that during their OBE they perceived a totally different place. In my opinion these individuals were not reporting an OBE but a lucid dream.

The major difference between an OBE and a lucid dream is that in most cases lucid dreamers find themselves in an environment other than their actual physical location. In other words an experiencer has the sensation of leaving their body (soma) and moving into the external space surrounding the soma. They still feel located in a physical space and, in some cases, within a form of etheric body, something I would like to term the 'ecsoma'.

The implication is that something has moved out of the soma and is located in real space close to the soma. The experiencer views the 'real' world through the senses of the ecsoma and can move around this environment as they would ordinarily do in normal life. Indeed, it is regularly reported that OBEs are so subtle that the experiencer simply thinks they have got up to go to another location such as the bathroom. It is only when they look back and see their soma that they realize they are in an ecsomatic state. This is known as a 'false awakening'. Some individuals report that this can happen two or three times. They wake up, go to the bathroom, something odd happens, they realize they are dreaming and wake up, go to the bathroom again and repeat the process, waking again and again until they really do find themselves in consensual reality.

False-awakening OOB states feel real because they are mundane. There is no feeling of strangeness until the experiencer spots the soma. However the more usual OOB state involves the ecsoma floating above the soma, usually looking down from a location near the ceiling. This is so odd that the experiencer becomes immediately aware that something peculiar is taking place. In consensual reality we do not view the world from a floating position near a ceiling. However strange this may feel, the experiencer is, as in the false-awakening scenario, located in a recognizable space, identical to a known location in consensual reality.

Twemlow's results, however, suggest that a significant minority of OBEs report the ecsoma in a completely different location from that of its soma. The interesting point here is how the ecsoma travels instantly from one location to another without being aware of making the journey. It is as if we have a series of different experiences being reported. One involves a gradual separation of soma and ecsoma, with the ecsoma moving normally within the consensual reality surrounding it. A second type involves the manifestation of consciousness into a location floating above the soma; in this case there is no gradual moving apart but an immediate waking-state in which the ecsoma is suddenly aware of being out-of-body. Let us recall that Robert Monroe described how, on dozing off to sleep, he suddenly finds himself fully awake again:

> My senses fully alert, I tried to see in the dim light. It was a wall, and I was lying against it with my shoulder. I immediately reasoned that I had gone to sleep and fallen out of bed. (I had never done so before, but all sorts of strange things were happening, and falling out of bed was quite possible.) Then I looked again. Something was wrong. This wall had no windows, no furniture against it, no doors. It was not a wall in my bedroom. Yet somehow it was familiar. Identification came instantly. It wasn't a wall, it was the ceiling. I was floating against the ceiling, bouncing gently with any movement I made. I rolled in the air, startled, and looked down. There, in the dim light below me, was the bed. There were two figures lying in the bed. To the right was my wife. Beside her was someone else. Both seemed asleep. This was a strange dream, I thought.

> I was curious. Whom would I dream to be in bed with
> my wife? I looked more closely, and the shock was
> intense. I was the someone on the bed![37]

He reports no sensation of a gradual leaving of his body. He just suddenly wakes up in a different place, a place that initially confused him because he had never experienced bouncing against a ceiling before. But Monroe was still in a location he recognized. He was still in his bedroom, albeit in an odd place in that bedroom.

To my mind, Monroe's experience is almost identical to those reported during near-death experiences. The person is suddenly located above their body and can observe what is going on around them. Both situations involve states in which the brain is unconscious, through trauma (during an accident), sedation (during an operation) or simply, as in Monroe's case, by being asleep.

Twemlow's minority group experiences a totally different environment and location from that of the soma. These experiences are suggestive of remote viewing rather than near-death experiences or false awakenings. This seems quite a different phenomenon, and one that is far closer to lucid dreaming.

So what exactly is lucid dreaming and how is it facilitated?

Lucid Dreaming

A lucid dreamer is somebody who has, by accident or by training, managed to become aware of the fact that they are dreaming during a dream state. Up to that point it is as if consciousness has been simply observing a dream sequence as an audience member observes a movie. Actually it is more complex than this. For most of us a dream experience seems totally real. We are viewing the dream from a first-person viewpoint, and are enclosed by the dream environment in exactly the same way that the world surrounds us in waking life. However, this is not like waking life. We can experience the oddest events, but we simply accept them. We can fly, meet odd creatures, and we perceive these things in a peculiar 'dreamscape' that can be totally at odds with the 'real' world of consensual reality. But at no time does the oddness make us aware that we are dreaming. For a lucid dreamer things are different. By using certain techniques a lucid dreamer can suddenly become aware of being in a dream-state. I wonder if we experience this in waking life when we sometimes get glimpses of another, deeper reality. Is this us 'waking up' within our ongoing 'waking dream' as suggested by a whole series of modern movies such as *Waking Life*, *Fight Club* and *Vanilla Sky*? The lucid dreamer seems to move from being an observer of a dream to that of an observer observing the observer of a dream, if that makes any sense. It is a sudden change of perceptual location. Not in real space but in psychic space.

In making this perceptual shift the lucid dreamer moves from a role of passive observer of dream events to a controller of dream events. They acquire almost god-like skills through which they can manipulate the world around them.

What they regularly report is that perceptions are heightened during a lucid dream. The environment encountered is imbued with a reality far greater than a normal dream. Now what is of significance to me is that 93 per cent of Twemlow's respondents claimed that their OBE was 'more real than a dream'.

This is a very important comment. The perception that the experience was 'more real than a dream' does not presuppose that the experience was not a dream, but simply a more vivid version of a dream. There is another factor relating to the OOB state that has not been picked up by writers on the subject, that is, the experiencer is aware of having an unusual experience. In other words they are self-aware during the experience. This state of self-awareness, together with hyper-intense perceptions, are the reasons why both experiencers and researchers consider the OOB state to be different from a dream state. But for me, these clues suggest the contrary – that the OBE is a lucid dream state.

As mentioned above, a self-aware lucid dreamer can manipulate his or her dream world with powers that are unthinkable in consensual reality. Indeed, many practised lucid dreamers use these abilities to confirm that they are in such a state. Robert Waggoner, an accomplished lucid dreamer and author of a fascinating book on the subject,[38] explained to me recently that he could, to a fair degree, control his dream environment and make it 'plastic'. Further, although many of the beings he encounters in this dream state are clearly projections of his mind, some, in his opinion, are not. He explained to me that in one lucid dream he saw in front of him a group of people wearing large hats. He flew over them and took great pleasure in knocking off the hats. This action gained no reactions until one of the 'beings', put his hand up to stop Waggoner hitting his hat and then purposefully ducked to avoid the impact. This showed pre-meditated action and self-volition on the part of the being.

Earlier I mentioned the similarities between Tom Campbell's NPMR and PMR and the popular web-based life simulation called *Second Life*. It will therefore come as no surprise that I also have noted huge parallels with *Second Life* and both lucid dreaming and ecsomatic experiences. Many millions of people are now experiencing an alternative life in this huge virtual world that has been created in cyberspace. The new member enters *Second Life* in a way that is similar to the experience of a lucid dream. On logging in, 'viewers' find themselves looking through their computer screen into a wonderfully rendered virtual world. In this world they can move about and discover things in the same way as they do in 'first' life.

This world is perceived from a first-person perspective looking at this world through the eyes of a being called an 'avatar'.

It is significant that the 'viewpoint' can be changed so a viewer can look through the eyes of the avatar or can position themselves a few feet behind and above the avatar's 'body'. This is very reminiscent of many classic ecsomatic experiences, such as that of Suzanne Segal discussed earlier. What is even more significant is that the viewer soon realizes they can fly within this new world. By thinking it – or more accurately by pressing a particular key on the computer keyboard – they can elevate the avatar into the air and then fly off in any direction. This is again very similar to virtually every report of lucid dreaming and many reports of near-death experience.

Clearly, *Second Life* is a world created by the minds of programmers using computer code. This digital world is built by line after line of binary sequences, which ultimately 'create' a three-dimensional facsimile of the 'real' world of 'First Life'. Many will argue that the 'real' world is also a mind-created digital illusion. This proposal therefore suggests that *Second Life* is simply an illusion within an illusion. Indeed, I am reminded of those nested Russian dolls in which each contains another doll. As we shall discover later, American quantum physicist David Bohm anticipated exactly such a scenario when he suggested that, at its deepest level, the universe is enfolded within itself in something he termed the *holomovement*.

I have discussed this *Second Life* analogy with friends who are regular visitors to that digital world. When I described to them the sensations experienced by lucid dreamers, they nodded in recognition. One described feeling as if he was entering an alternative state of consciousness on entering *Second Life*.

I would now like to return to the Tom Campbell model and how it can be applied to lucid dreaming. You will recall that Campbell worked with Robert Monroe and has since created his own model of reality that involves an interaction between what he terms physical matter reality (PMR) and non-physical matter reality or NPMR. In his trilogy of books, collectively entitled *My Big Toe*,[39] Campbell suggests that both PMR and NPMR are actually elements of a huge computer program, which 'creates' the perceived world in the same way that the humble PC renders a first-person virtual-reality computer game. When I discussed this with Tom recently I was immediately reminded of *Second Life*. In his lectures Tom discusses how the program (run on something he semi-jokingly refers to as the TBC – 'The Big Computer') works on similar principles in that, to save processing time, 'reality' as perceived by any 'observer' is only rendered in the direction of attention of that observer.

So, for example, within your present version of PMR the only information rendered is what you can see with your eyes. Your peripheral vision, which will look blurred as you look forward, contains less rendered information than what is in front of you. What is behind you is literally nothing. As you turn your head it 'pops' into existence only to disappear again when you look away. If Tom Campbell is correct, then we are existing within nested illusory realities, where the dream state is one of many. In this way dreams, lucid or otherwise, are as 'real' as consensual reality which, in turn, is an externally generated illusion.

WILDS and DILDS

One of the most fascinating books on lucid dreaming that I have read is Thomas Yuschak's *Advanced Lucid Dreaming – The Power of Supplements*. Yuschak is a very experienced lucid dreamer and, like many others, he is intrigued by the similarities between the LD experience and ecsomatic states such as the NDE and the OBE.

According to Yuschak there are two types of lucid dreams. He

explains that within the terminology of LD enth
called 'DILDs' (dream-induced lucid dreams) and '
induced lucid dreams).

A DILD is the classic lucid dream in that the pers⎯ ⎯⎯⎯⎯es
aware whilst already dreaming that they are in a dream state. A
WILD involves an immediate change from waking state to lucid-
dream state, with no transition and no loss of consciousness. This
transition is usually accompanied by, as Yuschak describes it, 'some
intense sensations such as a feeling of floating, strong vibrations,
and/or rapid accelerations'.[40]

Yuschak believes that when he experiences a WILD and leaves
his body in a state identical to that of an OBE, he is fairly sure
the room he finds himself in is a facsimile of the real room and
that it is created and modelled by his mind. This illusion facilitates
the unbroken transition from the fully-awake state to that of the
lucid-dream state as encountered in a WILD. He points out that this
happens in 40 per cent of his WILDs.

In another transition state during a WILD he describes how his
body seems to be accelerated towards the location where the WILD
will take place.

Another important point is that he regularly describes how he
sees his body in the LD and how everything is not at all 'dreamlike'.
If you read the articles suggesting that LDs and OBEs are different,
these are two of the elements that are cited as classic differentials;
another being that in a lucid dream there is no transition state – the
dreamer just finds themselves somewhere – but clearly this is exactly
what this writer does not experience. He has a very clear transition
state, identical in every way to an OBE, including the lifting out of
the body and seeing it on the bed.

He also makes the point that in a WILD there is a continuity
of awareness and that the lucid dreamer is fully aware of their

personality and memories. They know exactly who they are and their memory history. He states: 'Lucid dreamers consider this to be a transition into a dream whereas Astral Travellers believe it is real.'[41]

This is a very important point. In a fascinating description of this transition state, Yuschak describes how sometimes he feels as if he is 'rolling over' and then finds himself floating at a point near the ceiling. Does this not remind you of Monroe's 'rolling-over technique'? You may recall that when Robert encountered his first fully ecsomatic state he found himself in a similar position to that described by Yuschak – bouncing off the ceiling of his bedroom.

Indeed, many of Yuschak's descriptions remind me of Robert's encounters. In *Journeys Out of the Body*, Monroe describes a vivid 'semi-dream' in which he found himself feeling the rug on his bedroom floor, describing his amazement as his fingers went through the floor and into the floor below. On doing so he felt the rough upper surface of the ceiling of the room below. He then felt a small triangular piece of wood, a bent nail and some sawdust. On first encountering this description, it is easy to evaluate it as evidence of a genuine out-of-body perception of objects that actually exist in consensual reality. The bent nail and wood chip are exactly what one would expect to find in an area between floorboards and ceiling boards. However, and this is the important point, the very fact that one would expect such things to be there, may also suggest that this is some form of dream created out of expectations. That this may have been the case is evidenced by what happened next:

> I pushed my hand still deeper. It went through the first
> floor ceiling and I felt as if my whole arm was through
> the floor. My hand touched water. Without excitement,
> I splashed the water with my fingers.[42]

This is described by Robert as an out-of-body experience, yet clearly it is not. I cannot believe that there happened to be a pool of water, hovering at the top of the room below, and so deep that that he could splash it with his fingers. In my opinion this was obviously a lucid-dream state. Indeed, I am somewhat surprised that Monroe did not take the opportunity to prove his ecsomatic perceptions by having the bedroom floorboards raised to see if a bent nail and a triangular piece of wood were actually there as his experience suggested.

So what evidence is there for my belief that the lucid-dream state and the out-of-body experience are aspects of the same phenomenon?

Lucid Dreaming and the Out-of-Body State

In 1984 Stuart Twemlow and his associate Glen Gabbard[43] followed on from their 1982 study with a review of the perceived differences between the two phenomena. Firstly, they point out that lucid dreaming is far more common than the OBE. They claim that between 50 to 70 per cent of the population will experience a lucid dream, whereas only 14 to 20 per cent will experience an OBE. I personally find both sets of figures suspiciously high. I know of only a handful of individuals who lucidly dream as described in the literature. I know many who report 'vivid' dreams but that is an altogether different concept.

Secondly, they focus on the two lucid-dream states that we encountered earlier, namely DILDs (dream-induced lucid dreams) and WILDS (wake-induced lucid dreams). The former occur during REM sleep; the latter occur right at the beginning of sleep, within the hypnagogic state. Gabbard and Twemlow point out that some OOB states take place when somebody is awake. A good example of this is the case of Suzanne Segal. However, as we have seen, REM intrusion could explain these cases very adequately. This known phenomenon causes the individual to enter a dream state while thinking they are still awake. In effect this is another way of describing a lucid dream.

Thirdly, Twemlow and Gabbard focus on the subjective perceptive differences reported by the experiencers during altered states of consciousness. Some of these need to be commented upon. For example, one of the differences is that lucid dreamers have an integrated body image, whereas OBErs feel that they are separated from their everyday body (soma). In my understanding the reason for this is a simple one – lucid dreamers immediately find themselves in another location, a totally different location from that of their soma. Therefore, it is not surprising that they do not 'see' the soma in a lucid dream. Whilst in this state, they seem to perceive a sense of 'body image' as they would normally do in waking life. OBErs, on the other hand, usually report realizing that they are outside of their soma by seeing their body lying on a bed, at the roadside, on an operating table etc. But may this simply be a question of imposed definitions? The hypnagogic and hypnopompic states are really the same phenomenon that places consciousness in that liminal region between sleep and wakefulness. The only difference is the circumstances. The hypnagogic state is experienced on going to sleep and the hypnopompic state is experienced on waking up. We define an OBE when the subject is aware of their soma, and a lucid dream when the subject is unaware of their soma.

It is suggested that lucid dreamers are fully aware that the experience is a production of their minds, whereas OBErs consider the experience to be objective reality. I have to agree that this is a fair point, but could this be to do with the fact that lucid dreamers spend time trying to develop this skill? As such, when a lucid dream state is experienced it is not such a surprise. The lucid dreamer knows what to expect and is aware of being in a dream state. Is that not what we mean by the word 'lucid'? OBErs, on the other hand, are individuals who suddenly find themselves in this state. They have not planned it and have no way of interpreting what is happening to them; they suddenly find themselves in a totally alien location. Is this why it feels real? As I have never experienced either state, all I know is that my dreams always feel real to me as I experience them. This is a totally logical statement because, at the moment I realize that I am dreaming, my dream will, by definition, become lucid.

I also cannot avoid the fact that however real OBErs think that their experience is, the evidence from veridical experiments suggests otherwise. As I have stated throughout this book, if an ecsomatic state really is an experience in which a person's consciousness is located somewhere else, how come those tested consistently fail to identify things that would be simple in normal consensual reality?

For me, lucid dreaming is one of the most exciting areas of human experience and one that I genuinely believe will facilitate a new understanding regarding the nature of consciousness and its relationship with 'reality'.

Indeed, I consider that the lucid-dreaming phenomenon has great relevance to my own work in attempting to show that my own *Cheating the Ferryman* hypothesis, presented in my two previous books, has validity.

On my Forum at www.anthonypeake.com/forum my readers post their experiences. I have no rigid rules on what should be posted, but in general they will relate to one or more aspects of my 'CTF' hypothesis. Just as I had embarked upon the writing of this book, a regular 'poster' called Ian Wilson placed a series of comments that show just how powerful lucid dreaming can be.

Over the years Ian has experienced many precognitive dreams. Such a phenomenon has been known for centuries and in the 1930s an engineer by the name of JW Dunne presented a cogent philosophy as to how such processes may work. He suggested that in order for us to appreciate that time 'flows', there has to be a way that this time can be measured. All measuring processes involve gauging one thing against another. We use a ruler to measure length or a set of scales to measure weight. Flow is similarly measured by comparing it against a static object. For example, a river's flow is measured as its relative speed in relation to a static riverbank. If there were no riverbank, then we would have no way of even knowing that the river was flowing at all. But time is different. We can only measure time's flow by using time itself. We cannot quantify the duration of a minute except by measuring it against the flow of a second hand against a clock face, or by the changes on a digital display. But a moment's reflection will make us realize that duration and time are the same thing. This is what Dunne observed and he suggested that there must be a second time by which we measure time; and, by implication, a third form of time by which the second time is measured. Clearly this implies an infinite regress, but this did not concern Dunne. He also suggested that within each time is an 'observer' who observes this duration. From this he extrapolated that during sleep our everyday observer (who he called 'Observer One') can access the awareness of 'Observer Two', whose time perception is much broader. In other words, the 'present' for Observer Two may stretch out for a few days, or even weeks. This element of ourselves is aware of the contents of our immediate future. This is how he explained dream precognitions. Our dreams contain elements of our own future and, under certain circumstances, we can recall these precognitive elements; in doing so we 'precognize' the future. However, what is more usual is that we only recognize a dreamed future event as we start to encounter it in waking life. We have a sudden recognition and a dim recollection that this moment has been experienced before. This idea has been updated by Swiss-based American physicist and Jungian psychoanalyst Dr Arthur Funkhouser. Funkhouser calls this the 'Dream Theory of Déjà Vu'.

This is what has been happening to Ian Wilson. Over the years many of his dreams have come true. However, in recent years he has done something quite unique, and of profound significance. He has taught himself how to lucid dream. Now this may not, at first, seem of any great significance, but by becoming lucid in a dream Ian can manipulate it. And there is more. If that dream is a precognitive dream, then Ian can actively manipulate the external world within his own future.

He calls this process 'mapping' and he has had recorded success in using it to manipulate his own reality in such a way that it has not only been observed by others, but photographed as well.

Ian was experiencing a normal dream. By a normal dream I mean one in which we simply observe the events. Something triggered Ian into a state of awareness in which he knew that he was dreaming. He was then in a fully lucid state. He looked round and realized that he was in his current workplace. Behind a counter was one of his associates. The environment was so like that of the location in consensual reality, it suddenly dawned on Ian that this dream could have precognitive potential. He decided that he would make something happen in the dream that may come to pass in the future. However, it had to be something that could be visible and possibly measurable. Seemingly without thinking, he lifted his arm, pointed his finger, and made a triangle appear on the forehead of his work associate. As this was a dream, this was not surprising. However, in his lucid state, Ian was fully aware that such a thing was an impossibility within the science of consensual reality. Soon afterwards he awoke and the dream faded as many dreams do. However, Ian was aware that he had done something of significance whilst in his dream state.

A few weeks later he was reminded of what it was. In an interview in *Lucid Dream Exchange Magazine* Ian explained to Robert Waggoner what took place:

> About three weeks later, the lucid dream actualized. Like my first lucid precognitive dream, I felt an amazing synchronicity and déjà-vu-like aura as waking time and space synchronized with the lucid precognitive dream. In this reality, I stood six feet away from this person and I simply went with the flow of the lucid dream. My hand just lifted and the triangle formed as it did in the dream, perfectly on his head. It was visible enough for others to clearly see it. I remember him looking at me, as I pointed at him. Then he asked me, after the fact, what I did. I told him I placed a triangle on his head. A cashier next to him saw it, then she screamed and ducked behind the counter. He ran to the bathroom and looked at it in the mirror. When he came out he was definitely shocked at the visible mark. I took a Polaroid and another follow-up picture of it to have physical evidence of the experimentation. Later he wrote a statement of the account. Also he had to explain the mark to his mother who asked him how he got that strangely shaped bruise on his forehead. She saw it clearly. There was no question this was a very profound event for all of us involved.[44]

What is fascinating about this event is that, unlike many of the experiments and experiences described in this book, this case actually has supporting witness statements and photographs taken at the time, which clearly show the red mark on the face of Ian's associate.

The implications are of profound significance. What this suggests is that reality (consensual or subjective) is open to direct influence by a conscious mind. But this case is even stranger, because it suggests that Ian influenced the contents of his own future by making the gesture in his dream. Indeed, one could further suggest that Ian's whole dream was precognitive in that the gesture and the appearance of the mark already existed in Ian's future and all the dream did was reproduce that future. In other words, Ian had no choice other than to make that gesture in the dream because it too was part of the precognition. The implications of this are staggering. It suggests that Tom Campbell is quite right when he states that the inner world of non-physical material reality (NPMR) and the outer, shared world, of physical material reality (PMR) are just two sides of the same coin. Consciousness, or more specifically, the act of attention, is what creates both.

I was rapidly coming to conclude that in exactly the same way that NPMR and PMR are aspects of the same phenomenon, so it is that the OOB state is, in fact, identical to that of the classic lucid dream. I was interested to know what some of the major players in the world of ecsomatic experiences would think of this conclusion. I was also keen to see if the leading researchers and experiencers of both phenomena agreed with my opinion. I had extended discussions with Tom Campbell, Robert Waggoner and Australian astral traveller Robert Bruce and was both surprised and delighted to discover that we all shared the same opinion, that not only are the phenomena related but, they are simply the same experience perceived in slightly different ways. In simple terms, a very real experience in which consciousness is given access to a greater reality that exists deep within the structures of the brain.

In order for you to appreciate fully how my model works I now need to introduce you to the science behind consciousness, the wonders of quantum physics and the deep mysteries of mind-altering drugs. We will now devote the second half of this book to explain the events and experiences described in the first half.

The real adventure is just about to begin.

Part II
The Science

CHAPTER 8

Neurology

Hypnagogic Imagery and REM Intrusion

Over the last 20 years or so, I have developed very strong hypnagogic states. These happen most nights and involve the most bizarre imagery that manifests totally outside of my control. I cannot manipulate the images and they come and go in a way similar to watching a movie. The 'images' are 'out there' in space rather than within my mind's eye and they show a wilfulness that sometimes has me believing they are not part of my mind but that they are being created from elsewhere. Indeed, my first really vivid hypnagogic image was so powerful that I can still visualize it in my mind's eye.

Just as I was dropping off to sleep I found myself somewhere else, somewhere that clearly was not my bedroom. I seemed to be a point of consciousness floating about 12 feet above the ground. As I looked down I could see the top of somebody's head. The head was bald with wisps of hair around the side. It was an elderly gentleman sitting on what looked like a park bench. He was reading a large, broadsheet newspaper. The weather was very warm and something inside me knew that this was somewhere south, Spain or maybe Latin America. All the time I was viewing this scene I was self-aware. It was not a dream and did not feel like a dream. It was very real. I felt that I was actually there. I then found that my viewpoint was changing. I moved away from the vertical view looking down at the old gentleman and slowly levelled off into a horizontal position. This movement was at no time under my control; it was, again, as if I was immersed in a three-dimensional movie or hologram. As I moved, the view changed and I was able to take in a much broader vista. I could see that I was in the centre of a huge square in the middle of a very busy city; the square was surrounded by a road with lots of traffic. I could hear the beeping of horns and the continual hum of the traffic. The buildings on the other side of the road were large and imposing but had a slight air of dereliction. This was not a city I had ever been to but it felt like a very real place. I then heard the sound of a siren off to my right and watched as a white ambulance, lights flashing, weaved its way through the traffic. It was at this point that the whole image disappeared; it did not fade, it just switched off. But what was odder was my immediate state of mind. For the duration of the 'vision' I had had no state of selfhood. I was simply pure being. It was only when I came back that I again regained the person known as Anthony Peake. It was a very odd sensation but one that I decided to keep to myself.

A few weeks later it happened again. This time I was looking up through a glass table watching a grandly dressed middle-aged woman with a huge pink hat, placing a cup and saucer down on the transparent table. My initial thought was 'what an odd angle', but yet again I had no sense that it was 'Anthony Peake' doing the observing. This experience did not last as long as the first one and the image faded within seconds. Indeed, as time developed and I had more of these 'hallucinations', I realized that I had to 'view' them from a state of dissociation. The moment I became self-aware of me as an observer they stopped.

Quite by chance, I came across a reference to a phenomenon known as hypnagogic imagery. I discovered that I was not alone and that a small minority of people shared my nocturnal 'visions'. I found that some, like me, experience them just as they go to sleep and others on awaking; hypnopompic imagery is the term for the same sensation as the subject wakens from sleep.

I now have these hallucinations regularly but never at the intensity of the first two, images of which are still as strong now as they were on the nights they took place all those years ago. Indeed, I have long wondered about the location of the 'Spanish' city. On visiting Madrid a few years ago, I had a vague tinge of recognition when I stayed in an apartment next to a large, city-centre square. This square reminded me of my hypnagogic place but it was not really accurate. However, I am still sure that it is a real place.

The images that we perceive during a hypnopompic or hypnagogic state are clearly generated by the subconscious mind whilst consciousness itself hovers in that liminal place between being awake and asleep. It is as if dream images push their way into the waking world and, in doing so, allow us a glimpse of the place where lucid dreamers go throughout the night. Could it be that what is happening is that the brain is already sleeping whilst the mind is still awake? If this is the case then the state known as REM may be able to shed some light onto this mysterious state.

The acronym REM stands for 'rapid eye movement', a period during the sleep cycle of human beings (and some animals) when the eyes are seen to be rapidly moving from side to side underneath the eyelid. This phenomenon was first noticed by Eugene Aserinsky, a graduate student of the University of Chicago in the early 1950s. Aserinsky was monitoring the sleep patterns of young babies when he noticed that, at certain times during the sleep cycle, the baby's eyes suddenly started rapid movements, whereas at other times they showed no movement at all. Working with a fellow student, Nathaniel Kleitman, he expanded his studies to adults. However, changing. I moved away from the vertical view looking down at the old gentleman and slowly levelled off into a horizontal position. This movement was at no time under my control; it was, again, as if I was immersed in a three-dimensional movie or hologram. As I moved, the view changed and I was able to take in a much broader vista. I could see that I was in the centre of a huge square in the middle of a very busy city; the square was surrounded by a road with lots of traffic. I could hear the beeping of horns and the continual hum of the traffic. The buildings on the other side of the road were large and imposing but had a slight air of dereliction. This was not a city I had ever been to but it felt like a very real place. I then heard the sound of a siren off to my right and watched as a white ambulance, lights flashing, weaved its way through the traffic. It was at this point that the whole image disappeared; it did not fade, it just switched off. But what was odder was my immediate state of mind. For the duration of the 'vision' I had had no state of selfhood. I was simply pure being. It was only when I came back that I again regained the person known as Anthony Peake. It was a very odd sensation but one that I decided to keep to myself.

A few weeks later it happened again. This time I was looking up through a glass table watching a grandly dressed middle-aged woman with a huge pink hat, placing a cup and saucer down on the transparent table. My initial thought was 'what an odd angle', but yet again I had no sense that it was 'Anthony Peake' doing the observing. This experience did not last as long as the first one and the image faded within seconds. Indeed, as time developed and I had more of these 'hallucinations', I realized that I had to 'view' them from a state of dissociation. The moment I became self-aware of me as an observer they stopped.

Quite by chance, I came across a reference to a phenomenon known as hypnagogic imagery. I discovered that I was not alone and that a small minority of people shared my nocturnal 'visions'. I found that some, like me, experience them just as they go to sleep and others on awaking; hypnopompic imagery is the term for the same sensation as the subject wakens from sleep.

I now have these hallucinations regularly but never at the intensity of the first two, images of which are still as strong now as they were on the nights they took place all those years ago. Indeed, I have long wondered about the location of the 'Spanish' city. On visiting Madrid a few years ago, I had a vague tinge of recognition when I stayed in an apartment next to a large, city-centre square. This square reminded me of my hypnagogic place but it was not really accurate. However, I am still sure that it is a real place.

The images that we perceive during a hypnopompic or hypnagogic state are clearly generated by the subconscious mind whilst consciousness itself hovers in that liminal place between being awake and asleep. It is as if dream images push their way into the waking world and, in doing so, allow us a glimpse of the place where lucid dreamers go throughout the night. Could it be that what is happening is that the brain is already sleeping whilst the mind is still awake? If this is the case then the state known as REM may be able to shed some light onto this mysterious state.

The acronym REM stands for 'rapid eye movement', a period during the sleep cycle of human beings (and some animals) when the eyes are seen to be rapidly moving from side to side underneath the eyelid. This phenomenon was first noticed by Eugene Aserinsky, a graduate student of the University of Chicago in the early 1950s. Aserinsky was monitoring the sleep patterns of young babies when he noticed that at certain times during the sleep cycle, the baby's eyes suddenly started rapid movements, whereas at other times they showed no movement at all. Working with a fellow student, Nathaniel Kleitman, he expanded his studies to adults. However, unlike babies, adults find it more difficult to sleep in unusual circumstances, such as under the bright lights in a laboratory. To help decide if sleep was encroaching, they decided to wire their subjects to an electroencephalograph (EEG). Quite by chance they were then in a position also to observe brain activity when the eye movements started. Much to their surprise they found that this matched perfectly a change in the electrical activity of the brain. From the typical sleep state, the activity changed to that of a fully awake person as soon as the REM started. As Kleitman later described it, 'These changes suggested some sort of emotional disturbance, such as might be caused by dream'. This proved to be a very perceptive comment. With their associate, Bill Demmont, the two researchers agreed that the best way to prove Kleitman's suspicion was to wake the subjects as soon as the REM episode started. The results were encouraging: 70 per cent of those awoken in this way reported dreaming just before they were roused.

Since that time, the association between REM activity and dreaming has been solidly confirmed, but it was only in 2007 that a new angle on this topic was presented to the scientific community. A paper entitled 'Out of the Body Experiences and Arousal' by Kevin Nelson, Michelle Mattingly, Sherman Lee and Frederick Schmitt was published in the April edition of the journal *Neurology*. In this paper the researchers presented evidence that the REM phenomenon could be directly linked to ecsomatic states.

The researchers have termed this experience 'REM Intrusion'. They suggest that there can be circumstances in which a person may *think* that they are awake but are, in fact, not only asleep but in a REM dream state. They suggest two forms. The first is sleep paralysis. This is where the person feels that they are paralysed and, in some cases, that they cannot breathe. The second form involves sleep-related hallucinations, such as the hypnagogic and hypnopompic experiences I describe happening to me earlier in the chapter.

Could REM Intrusion be used to explain the curious ecsomatic states recorded by the International Academy of Consciousness at their research campus in Portugal? You will recall that volunteers were placed in states of sensory deprivation in the facilities known as the Projectarium and the Immobilitarium. After a few hours in this state many volunteers reported leaving their body and visiting other locations. Could these experiences be attributed to the brain creating a condition in which the person is sleeping but still conscious?

If this is correct, then it suggests that the brain itself may store memories in a format whereby they can be reproduced and played back in a similar way to a movie or a DVD. As a result there should be evidence that the brain can perform this process when stimulated to do so.

Olaf Blanke and Ecsomatic Perceptions

In 2002 a revolutionary procedure took place in a hospital in Switzerland. The patient was a 43-year-old woman who had suffered severe epileptic seizures for 11 years. The surgeons had implanted over 100 electrodes across the patient's skull, allowing the doctors to electronically stimulate various areas of her brain and, in doing so, draw a very detailed map of her brain activity and functioning. One particular electrode had been placed above the right temporal lobe of the patient. Adjacent to this area is a location known as the angular gyrus, which is known to be responsible for language, mathematics and cognition.

When this particular electrode was activated, the woman immediately reported that she was floating above her own body and looking down at herself. As the electrodes are only switched on for two seconds at a time, the doctors were able to quickly switch to another electrode located elsewhere in her brain. When they did so, the ecsomatic experience stopped. They then tested the effect by going back to the angular gyrus electrode to see if the effect was repeated. It was. It was clear that the woman was not faking this sensation. Any one of over 100 electrodes could be activated, but she correctly reported the out-of-body sensation only when that specific electrode was activated.

This result intrigued one of the neurologists involved, Dr Olaf Blanke. He had been involved in applying this procedure over a period of seven years and had never come across such a peculiar response. He was sure that this was to do with the way in which the brain processes body position and location. He came to this conclusion because in the same session, again when the same electrode was activated, the woman screamed with fear and claimed that she 'saw' her legs shortening and 'saw' her knees about to hit her face.

It has long been known that the angular gyrus is also responsible for spatial awareness, so, as far as Blanke was concerned, the electrode had brought about confusion in how the angular gyrus processed the patient's awareness of her body's position in space. Stimulated by this event, Blanke decided to attempt a reproduction of the circumstances under controlled laboratory conditions.

He concluded that the actual location of the effect was the right temporal-parietal junction (TPJ) and he decided to focus his work on this part of the cerebral cortex. Blanke's intention was to generate an ecsomatic sensation by scrambling the subject's tactile sensations and, in doing so, trick the brain into thinking that the body was somewhere else. He and his co-workers published their results in the science magazine *Nature* in 2002.[45]

Blanke continued his experiments at the École Polytechnique Fédérale in Lausanne, Switzerland. In an ingenious use of modern technology he had the subject sit on a chair; behind the subject was a video camera filming the view from behind. A 'virtual reality' headset was then placed over the subject's head. In the headset, and placed seemingly in the frontal visual field of the subject, was the image from the TV camera behind them. So in effect they were looking at their own back located in front of them. One of the experimenters would then stroke the back of the subject. The subject then had the sensation that they were no longer in their own body and that their consciousness had transferred itself to the illusory body in their own field of vision.

Of course this is a very peculiar position to be in. We are used to looking at ourselves in a mirror, but that image is reversed and actually facing us. In the Blanke experiment the projected body image was in exactly the same position as the subject's actual body. When the subject moved, so did the image, not as a mirror-image but as an accurate reproduction in space in front of the actual body.

He then added a further experiment whereby he blindfolded the volunteers immediately following the above procedure. He guided them a few steps backwards and then asked them to walk back to their original spatial location. Every subject became confused and walked forward to the location where the illusory body had been perceived rather than the actual location where the real body had been.

Blanke had, however, only partly reproduced the ecsomatic sensation. The subjects perceived themselves as out of their bodies but did not have the sensation of seeing their own body from that position. A similar experiment that took place at University College in London, under the guidance of Henrik Ehrsson of the Karolinska Institute of Stockholm, managed to reproduce this sensation as well.

Ehrsson reproduced a similar layout to Blanke but added the complexity of stereo binocular perception. Instead of one camera behind the volunteer there were two, placed next to each other and six feet behind the volunteer. The volunteer wore goggles connected to the two cameras; the left camera projected to the left eye and the right camera to the right eye. As a result, the volunteer saw their own back in a three-dimensional image from the perspective of a person sitting six feet behind them. An experimenter then stroked the chest of the volunteer with a stick for a period of two minutes. As this was happening, a second stick was moved in front and slightly below the camera lens. The position of the second stick was such that it would seem to be stroking a 'virtual' chest located in the same somatic position as the first stick was in relation to the volunteer's real chest. The volunteers had the sensation of not only being disembodied, but also that they were viewing their own body from a distance. Ehrsson seemed to have fully reproduced an ecsomatic sensation by artificial means.

Initially, I found these cases particularly effective as explanations of the neurological basis of the ecsomatic experience. However, a short period of reflection made me less convinced. In regard to the Blanke experiment, the subject failed to perceive the one crucial element that disturbs individuals who sense that they are outside of their soma – that they see their own body in front of them. I agree that Ehrsson did reproduce a similar sensation, but again, if this is considered objectively, he did not reproduce anything of the sort. The 'image' of the body in space was reproduced by a TV image. This image was a facsimile that was presented to the visual field of the volunteer. As such they 'saw' a TV image of their own body, nothing more. As far as I am aware, this does not account for the mechanism whereby, in a genuine ecsomatic experience, the subject, without the aid of a TV camera behind, still sees a body in three-dimensional space in front of them.

A further problem arises in that all the cases of ecsomatic experiences that I have read about, or that have been told to me by experiencers, the body left behind on the bed, or wherever, is not viewed from behind in exactly the same position as the 'astral body' is perceived to be. My fellow writer Herbie Brennan describes an experience that cannot be explained by either of the above experiments. He woke up and got out of bed to go to the toilet. As he looked back he saw somebody sleeping in the bed with his wife. He went back to the bed and realized that the person that was sleeping was himself. He looked at his own face above the blankets. Note, he was not looking at the back of his head and the body, in the bed was obviously in a very different position to Herbie's astral body, which was standing up and looking down. At the beginning of this book I cited the case of the soldier in Malaya. As he described the event on BBC Merseyside he was quite precise. He saw himself sitting on the bed facing the location where his 'astral body' was. Again, this was not in any way the same position that he felt he was in.

Therefore, I agree that the angular gyrus may be where this sensation is created, but not in the way proposed by Blanke and Ehrsson.

Interestingly, Blanke discovered that different sensations were perceived depending upon whether it was the left or right angular gyrus that was stimulated. When the right was manipulated, the subject felt as if she was floating near the ceiling facing downwards towards the floor. However, stimulation of the left angular gyrus brought about the sensation that there was a shadowy figure lurking just behind the subject.

This 'shadowy figure' is not unique to the work of Olaf Blanke; a similar perception was reported by the subjects of a series of experiments that took place at the Laurentian University in Sudbury, Canada, from the late 1980s onwards.

These controversial experiments by American cognitive neurologist Michael Persinger suggested that religious and mystic experiences could be generated by the stimulation of the temporal lobes of the brain. Persinger and his Canadian associates designed something that has now become popularly known as the 'God helmet'. This rather grand-sounding piece of headwear was, in fact, a modified snowmobile helmet containing a series of loops of wires that generated weak electromagnetic fields.

The helmet was placed on the head of the subject and the magnetic-field generating solenoids turned on. According to Persinger, at least 80 per cent of the subjects reported a very similar sensation to that of Blanke and Ehrsson's patients; an overwhelming feeling that there was a presence in the room with them. Others reported that they could perceive a shadowy, cowelled figure lurking within the extreme of their field of vision.

What is taking place when the brain is stimulated in this way? Clearly such stimulation is artificial in that external mechanisms are needed to bring about these altered states. However, it is also clear that these states are very 'real' as far as the subject or patient is concerned. At no time did any of the patients of Blanke or Persinger state they were aware that it was simply their mind 'playing tricks'. These were genuinely frightening perceptions, possible glimpses into an alternative reality where these beings have an existence of their own.

Such sensations and perceptions have been reported for centuries. People have encountered alien entities, some friendly and some malevolent. The process of encountering these alternative realities worked in a very similar way to the laboratory procedures of the late 20th century, but the routes to these altered states were not mechanical but chemical. It is to the world of mind-altering drugs that we now turn our attention in our search to understand the ecsomatic experience.

CHAPTER 9

The Psychedelic Route

As we have discussed, famous ecsomatic experiencer Robert Monroe stated that there are three locations the human mind can access during ecsomatic states. He called these 'Locales'. Locale 1 is the world we perceive with our everyday senses; it is the world that we share with others and seems constant and solid. In Locale 1, time is linear and flows from the future to the present and into the past. Locale 2 is the place where we all go in dreams and is heavily self-created, but still has an independent existence from the 'observer'. Locale 3 is the next level and is a place that seems physically real. Indeed, Monroe speculated that beings inhabiting this place live almost parallel lives to our own. He even suggested that in Locale 3 our own doppelgangers may be found, maybe many of them living slightly different lives on alternate planes of existence.

I am of the opinion that Monroe was, certainly, travelling to very real places and that his 'Locales' make logical sense when reviewed in the light of modern research into the nature and powers of mind-altering drugs. Could it be that when somebody moves into an 'altered state of consciousness' (ASC), either through a spontaneous change in brain processing or else due to the effects of psychedelics, that they actually enter one of Monroe's Locales?

In order to appreciate the strength of this argument we need to have a basic understanding of how the brain works, particularly in relation to its electrochemical processes.

The Gateway Port

No more than a few centimetres behind your eyes can be found the singularly most complex object in the universe – your brain. But how does it work its magic? Even now, in the first years of the 21st century, much about this wonderful piece of organic engineering is a mystery. We have no idea how it does many things, including the greatest mystery of all: how it brings about self-conscious awareness.

If one takes a section of brain material and views it through a powerful microscope, what is seen is a dense network of cells. Most of these will be what are called 'glial cells'. It seems that the role of these is simply to 'glue' the brain structure together and ensure it keeps its shape. However, dotted among these glial cells at a ratio of approximately 1 in 10 are neurons – cells that are adapted to send, receive and carry electrical impulses. Each neuron has a central, usually star-shaped, section where the cell nucleus is located. Spreading out from this central body are long, thin tendrils that can vary from between 1 millimetre and 1 metre in length. These tendrils reach out and can receive or send electrochemical signals from as many as 10,000 other neurons.

When a nerve cell is activated, or fired, an electrical current runs along the nerve fibre and releases a chemical substance called a neurotransmitter.

The existence of neurotransmitters, although long suspected, was confirmed in the 1930s, but it was only in the 1960s that their role was fully understood. To date, 50 or so have been isolated, the most important being serotonin, noradrenaline, glutamate and a group of pain-killing opiates called endorphins. These chemicals can have a marked effect upon mood and temperament. By stimulating the internal creation of these neurotransmitters, an individual's whole personality can be changed.

So how do they work? In simple terms, neurotransmitters are the chemical agents that are released by the neurons, to stimulate other neurons and, in the process, transmit impulses from one cell to the other. In turn this facilitates the transfer of messages throughout the whole nervous system. The site where neurons meet is called the synapse, consisting of the axon terminal (transmitting end) of one cell and the dendrite (receiving end) of the next. A microscopic gap called a synaptic cleft exists between the two neurons. When a nerve impulse arrives at the axon terminal of one cell a chemical substance is released through the membrane close to the synapse. This substance then travels across the gap, in a matter of milliseconds, to arrive at the post-synaptic membrane of the adjoining neuron. This chemical release is stimulated by the electrical activity of the cell. Across the other side of the cleft, at the end of the receiving dendrite, are specialized areas that act as docking zones for particular neuro-transmitters. These are known as 'receptors'. It is useful to visualize the receptors as docks at a port; sometimes they will be open to let in ships containing cargo and sometimes they will be closed and the ships cannot unload their goods.

If the newly arrived neurotransmitter chemical is allowed into the dock it is free to 'instruct' the dendrite to send a particular signal along to its nucleus then out to its own axons. When it does this it is said to be excitatory. Sometimes the effect of the neurotransmitter(s) released by the pre-synaptic axon is to inhibit rather than excite the post-synaptic dendrite. In this case it is said to be inhibitory.

Over the years, new chemicals were added to the list of substances that could act as neurotransmitters. Recently, however, a series of discoveries suggests that some neurotransmitters may have functions that indicate consciousness could access levels of awareness above and beyond the material world presented by the five senses.

The Glutamate/Ketamine Case

There are many different chemicals that act as neurotransmitters throughout the whole human nervous system. Glutamate is one of these specialist chemicals; technically speaking, it is the monoamide of glutamic acid. The majority of large neurons in the cerebral cortex use glutamate as their neurotransmitter. It is the key chemical messenger in the temporal and frontal lobes, and is central to the function of the hippocampus. Glutamate plays an essential role in the cognitive processes involving the cerebral cortex, including thinking and the formation of memories and their recall; it is vital in perception.

When brain cells start to die due to too little oxygen (hypoxia), a reduction in blood supply (ischaemia) and, significantly, during an epileptic seizure, they are stimulated to release large amounts of glutamate.[46]

Research carried out by Karl Jansen at the Maudsley Hospital in London[47] and his subsequent summation[48] supports his contention that the hallucinogenic anaesthetic ketamine can reproduce all the features of both the OBE and the closely related near-death experience. These include rapid trips down dark tunnels into light, seeing a being or beings, out-of-body experiences, mystic states and memory recall. In a monograph written on the general effects of psychedelic drugs, Jansen describes what the effects of ketamine involved:

> … becoming a disembodied mind or soul, dying and
> going to another world. Childhood events may also be
> relived. The loss of contact with ordinary reality and
> the sense of participation in another reality are more
> pronounced and less easily resisted than is usually the
> case with LSD. The dissociative experiences often seem
> so genuine that users are not sure that they have not
> actually left their bodies.[49]

It is interesting to note that childhood memories are part of the effects experienced whilst under the influence of ketamine.

Ketamine, once in the brain, attaches itself to a glutamate receptor called the N-methyl-D-aspartate or NMDA receptor for short. Continuing with our port analogy, it is useful to imagine these receptors to be like tiny harbours with several docks. What ketamine does, in effect, is blockade the harbour, thereby stopping any glutamate getting through to its receptors. Generally, glutamate is not harmful, but under certain circumstances vast amounts are generated, causing what is termed a glutamate flood. The circumstances that lead to a glutamate flood are times of extreme threat or crisis, particularly a life-threatening situation. However, it is counterproductive to have a potentially damaging flood of chemicals in the brain, particularly if the life-threatening situation proves to be a false alarm.

Evidence has shown that ketamine prevents neurotoxic damage by blockading the NMDA receptor and thus preventing glutamate spreading from cell to cell. As a psychedelic drug it also causes similar psychological effects as a typical NDE. Jansen believes that during a natural near-death event the glutamate flood is prevented by the internal generation of a substance that protects the NMDA receptors by binding to one of the 'docks' in the NMDA 'harbour'. This 'dock' is called the PCP receptor. This substance must, by its very nature, have an effect very similar to that of ketamine on the psychological state of the person involved. This endogenous (internally created) drug is the trigger for natural near-death experiences.

In 1984 endogenous substances were found in the brain that bind to the PCP receptor, and one of these was a peptide called alpha-endopsychosin.[50] Peptides are a peculiar group of neurotransmitters discovered in the 1970s. Initially found only in the intestine, it caused great surprise when they were also discovered in the brain. What was even more curious was that small amounts of one type (TRH) can induce euphoric states and has been used as an antidepressant. Another (beta-endorphin) causes muscular rigidity and immobility (catatonia) whilst the wonderfully named luteinizing-hormone-releasing-hormone (LHRH) is reputed to stimulate libido. Alpha-endopsychosin is a member of an ever-growing group of internally generated drugs that are called endogenous morphines (shortened to 'endorphins'). These are the body's own opiates, and as well as controlling pain they can also bring about euphoria and hallucinations. Until the discovery of alpha-endopsychosin, endorphins, although believed to be responsible in some way for NDEs,[51,52] were found to lack the potency needed to cause such powerful perception-altering effects. It has been shown that endorphins secreted as a response to stress have a sudden rise and a slow decay over several hours – probably longer than a typical NDE.

We now know that endopsychosins have exactly the same effect as ketamine in stopping the glutamate flood. As such, it is reasonable to believe that the conditions triggering an ecsomatic experience may also trigger an endopsychosin flood to protect cells. Therefore, the out-of-body experience could be considered to be a side effect caused by a purely physical reaction.

Developments have been made in the last ten years, with a series of little known discoveries, that suggest glutamate is not alone in this effect. An even more powerful way in which the brain may open up another door to parallel universes may have been found. In my opinion this may be one of the most significant discoveries of modern times, and may finally present us with a neurochemical explanation for the ecsomatic experience. These discoveries involve an intriguing molecule known as dimethyltryptamine.

In 1972, Nobel laureate chemist Julius Axelrod was analysing a sample of human brain tissue when he found a substance that had no reason to be there. It was called dimethyltryptamine and, as its name suggests, this chemical is a member of the amine family. Amines had been found to be important in the cells of invertebrates such as insects, but the amines were thought to have no function within the cells of higher animals such as mammals. In 1965, dimethyltryptamine had been found to be present in human blood, but to discover it in the human brain posed some very intriguing questions. This meant that it had some form of neurological function, which at that time was totally mysterious. As an amine it had no known receptors within the neurons and therefore could not be considered a neurotransmitter.

However, in 2001 a new family of receptors was found in the brains of all mammals. Tests had shown that they bind with, and are activated by, amines such as dimethyltryptamine. The existence of these trace amine-associated receptors (TAARs) confirmed the suspicion that trace amines acted as neurotransmitters within the mammalian brain.

In February 2009 a paper was published in the academic periodical *Science*. In this article Arnold Ruoho, the chair of pharmacology at the University of Wisconsin-Madison, described how his team had been searching for any molecules that would bind to a receptor known as sigma-1. Much to their surprise they discovered that this receptor is activated by dimethyltryptamine.[53]

The 37-year mystery had been solved. Dimethyltryptamine was found within the brain because it had an important role in the neurochemical functioning of the brain. If the sigma-1 receptor had evolved to allow access to this chemical, then one conclusion was inescapable – dimethyltryptamine is an internally generated neurotransmitter that has evolved within the brain for a specific purpose. The question that neurologists are now asking is what this purpose is.

The reason why the answer to this question is so fascinating is because of one well-known fact about dimethyltryptamine, DMT, as it is more popularly known – it is the most powerful hallucinogenic drug known to man, and our brains create it naturally. The question is, why?

Strassman and DMT

Mind-altering drugs have been known to human beings for hundreds, if not thousands, of years. Even the most isolated cultures seem to quickly discover what plants can supply psychedelic effects. However, without exception, such drugs are extracted from their source material through smoking or other chemical extraction processes. Clearly such substances are alien to the human body, and in particular the human brain. To smoke or otherwise ingest these drugs will be dangerous simply because the human body is not designed to cope with any side effects.

The human body, on the other hand, has evolved over hundreds of millions of years. It works like a well-oiled machine. All its components work together to ensure that everything runs smoothly. Of course, sometimes the body turns on itself, but that can usually be put down to external substances or life forms such as microbes or viruses causing a malfunction of the system. Every substance generated by the body has a purpose within the overall scheme of things.

Dimethyltryptamine was first isolated by a British chemist in 1931. At the time it was simply noted as another chemical substance, but 25 years later a Hungarian chemist by the name of Stephen Szara discovered that it had profoundly strong psychotropic properties. 'Psychotropic' is the scientific term for a much more popular term, 'mind altering'. This drug really could play with your mind in a way no other substance could.

Interestingly, DMT can be found naturally occurring on the skin of toads, specifically the cane toad of Central and South America. So if you really want to have a psychedelic experience all you need to do is lick a toad! I wonder whether this is the source of the stories about young women kissing frogs and finding that they turn into handsome princes?

But the most fascinating fact is that DMT has also been found to be the primary active ingredient of ayahuasca, a drink that has been used by Amazonian tribes for centuries to bring about profound out-of-body states and to facilitate communication with the gods.

It was information such as this that fascinated Dr Richard Strassman, an associate professor of psychiatry at the University of New Mexico Medical School. Dr Strassman was keen to understand exactly what was happening when DMT took control of consciousness. He had long suspected that when a person approaches death, the pineal gland releases DMT and in doing so brings about the classic near-death experience, specifically the ecsomatic elements of this enigmatic state.

As we have seen already, the pineal gland has been linked to ecsomatic experiences for centuries. In the late 19th century the founder of Theosophy, Helena Blavatsky, considered that this organ was of profound significance for the spiritual development of humankind, and in the 1920s Hereward Carrington and Sylvan Muldoon linked it directly to the ecsomatic state. As we have already discussed, it was the writings of Muldoon and Carrington that stimulated Tom Campbell and his associate Dennis Mennerich of the Monroe Institute to apply an electric field to this fascinating organ and in doing so develop something known as the HemiSync.

But for Strassman this was simply a neurochemical enquiry. Was the pineal gland involved in the production of DMT and how could this be measured?

First, he wished to analyse the psychological effects of externally sourced DMT on a group of human volunteers. In 1991 he embarked upon the first psychedelic research programme in the United States since 1970. He was given laboratory facilities at the New Mexico School of Medicine in Albuquerque. He had 60 volunteers and over a period of five years he administered 400 shots of DMT. Over this extended period he both observed and received feedback from the volunteers about what was taking place as the DMT took hold.

What he discovered was of great importance in our attempt to understand what is really taking place when somebody has an ecsomatic experience. Many of Strassman's volunteers reported the sensation of leaving the body and finding themselves in another location. This location was as real to them as the consensual world that they had left behind.

Strassman had expected this reaction. He was also not surprised to find that many of the subjects reported experiences very similar to the NDE. However, what he was not expecting was regular reports in which other, seemingly sentient and self-motivated beings, were encountered. These beings seem fascinatingly similar to the ones described by Robert Monroe when he was 'visiting' Locale 2, resembling elves or clowns and showing great interest in how the volunteers had ended up in this place. What was a particularly disturbing constant was that these entities made their presence felt after only a few seconds of the drug taking effect.

One of the consistent points made by out-of-body and remote-viewing practitioners is that the places they 'travel' to are absolutely real because they have no sensation of dreaming. The ecsomatic state is, as far as general perceptions go, identical to the normal world. Furthermore, they claim they are fully self-aware in these states. The point is made that in dream states or drug-induced hallucinations the sense of self is watered down or even lost, and the environment literally feels 'dream-like'; this was absolutely not reported by Strassman's volunteers. All of them insisted that their experience had taken place in a very real, three-dimensional location that was most definitely not a dream. They could walk around and explore; they did not feel in any way drunk or intoxicated. In fact, the general report was that they felt clarity of perception greater than in the 'waking world'.

Of course, as long as DMT was believed to be an alien chemical that had to be inhaled or injected, then, however intriguing the effects, they were still artificially induced. But the discovery of the trace amine receptors in 2001 and the binding properties of the sigma-1 receptor in 2009 have presented us with the hugely significant fact suggesting that DMT is an endogenous (internally generated) substance.

The implications for this are astounding. It is now a real possibility that all the ecsomatic types, the NDE, OBE, lucid dreaming and remote viewing, are natural states of consciousness, not hallucinations brought about by a sick or damaged brain. Furthermore, it is reasonable to suggest that the human brain has evolved in such a way that these brain states must have a purpose.

In an even more intriguing development, it has been suggested that all infants born naturally (rather than by Caesarean section) receive a mind-enhancing 'shot' of DMT at the moment of birth. It has also been suggested that the pineal gland becomes fully functional and capable of generating DMT on the 49th day of foetal development. Is this the point that consciousness enters the body? Coincidentally, or maybe not, the Buddhists also believe that the transmigrating soul spends 49 days in a trans-body state before it is 'reborn' into a new body.

What can we make of this? It is clear that DMT really does seem to open up some form of portal to another reality; a reality that seems to be consistent across the various out-of-body states. For me the parallels between the DMT induced hallucinations and Monroe's 'Locale 2' cannot be ignored.

Nonetheless, it is one thing to prove that these altered states of consciousness are generated by the brain, but quite another to suggest that they are in any way 'real'. Schizophrenics experience terrifying hallucinations, and even individuals who experience temporal lobe epilepsy and migraine report altered states of consciousness. These are similarly generated by an assortment of endogenous brain chemicals. Most people do not believe that these illusions are real. So what is different about DMT?

The Metatonin Case

Melatonin is the substance that encourages consciousness to sleep and, in doing so, allows the body to recharge itself. A related substance, metatonin, works in a similar but subtly different way. It allows us to hover at the borderline between sleep and wakefulness. Melatonin is secreted by the pineal gland and it has long been suspected that metatonin has the same source. The main active chemical of metatonin is DMT. It may therefore be of some significance that the Greek word for the pineal gland is *epiphysis* or epiphany.

The term metatonin is a new word suggested by researcher Beach Barrett. Barrett uses this term to describe internally created and therefore natural DMT, as opposed to the synthetic and illegal version that can be bought on the streets.

Usually the amount of metatonin within the brain is very carefully controlled. It is continually excreted but then destroyed by an enzyme known as monoamine oxidase or MAO.

For somebody who is unprepared, metatonin release can be extremely frightening. The body is in sleep state and paralysed by the melatonin effect, but the mind is awake and aware because of the modifying effect of the metatonin. For the person involved, this will be perceived as the phenomenon known as 'sleep paralysis', as discussed earlier.

It is relevant to note the position of the pineal gland within the brain; as it is at the very centre, it can quickly flood the surrounding areas with metatonin. During the start of an ecsomatic experience some people report that they have an acrid, metallic taste at the back of the throat. Barrett suggests that this may be related to the fact that, after the 49th day of gestation, the pineal gland develops in a location at the back of the throat; over a period of time it moves slowly up into the brain. However, in adults a small duct still remains. Barrett proposes that some of the excess metatonin may leak through a vestigial duct into the throat. He adds that in the Far East there are religious texts that describe something called 'the nectar of sublime awareness' that is produced during deep meditation

In a fascinating article on this subject (found on the Cottonwood Research website), Barrett makes a very interesting observation. He states that, preceding this overflow, the subject may feel 'a pulsing, whuffing sound/pressure wave that seems to come in from all sides'.[54] This reminds me strongly of Robert Monroe's description of his first ecsomatic experience as 'it was not a shaking, more a vibration, steady and unvarying in frequency. It felt much like an electric shock running through the entire body without the pain involved'.[55]

Barrett suggests seven different circumstances that initiate the release of metatonin. These are:

- extreme mental focus
- strong physical or emotional extremes
- periods of extreme pain
- near-death experiences
- lucid dreaming
- mental illness
- being a young child

I am particularly interested in the implications of the mental illness group. Barrett suggests that in this case the MAO production is not sufficient and the subject's brain is continually being flooded with metatonin. He points out that research in the 1970s showed that the level of metatonin was found to be higher than normal in the urine of schizophrenic patients. Clearly, at that time it was not known that metatonin was a neurotransmitter and this discovery was of potential significance.

However, in a paper written in 2008, Barrett makes the fascinating suggestion that the pineal gland may indeed be a portal into parallel realities. He proposes that this small organ could be a 'wormhole' that uses something called an 'Einstein-Rosen Bridge' to project consciousness into alternative universes.

Put simply, an Einstein-Rosen Bridge is a hole linking two areas of space-time. Imagine that space is flat like a sheet of paper. Imagine then a piece of paper 20 inches from top to bottom. If you fold the paper back on itself in a long 'U' shape and then push a pencil through from one side to the other, an inch down from the top, you have, in effect, shown the principle of these hypothetical structures. The pencil now acts as a link between two locations on the surface of the paper. If you fold the two surfaces together then the holes where the pencil enters the paper and subsequently exits are adjoining each other, the distance between them being just twice the thickness of the paper. If the pencil is then taken out and the paper laid flat, the two communicating holes caused by the pencil are suddenly 18 inches apart. As Einstein proposed that space-time was curved then such a scenario is a possibility.

Unfortunately these theoretical 'wormhole' structures are created by a black hole sucking matter through space-time and ejecting it at the other side in a structure known as a 'white hole'. As it is considered impossible for physical matter to travel through a black hole because of the intense gravitational forces, the idea that anything can cross space-time in this way is unfeasible.

However, consciousness is not made of matter and therefore would not be affected by the forces that would tear a physical object apart. If the vast areas of empty space found within the subatomic world within each atom of our brain are taken into account, then we all have, within us, curved space that may realistically contain micro black holes sucking in vast quantities of 'energy'. Similarly, tiny Einstein-Rosen Bridges could be created within this vast plenum.

Consciousness could access parallel universes by disappearing from this universe into another though a wormhole. Is this how Robert Monroe found himself in Locale 3?

But in order for this model to work we need to find out if such 'energy' exists. Is there a form of energy that fills empty space and turns it from a vacuum that, by definition, contains nothing, into a plenum – a place that is absolutely full and alive with potential?

A recent series of experiments have suggested that such a form of energy not only exists, but also fills all of space, both inner and outer. Called zero-point energy, this potentially unlimited source of fuel may solve all our present energy problems.

To understand why this discovery is of such significance in our quest to understand what is really happening in an out-of-the-body experience, we need to revisit a part of our education that many of us left behind in our teenage years – physics, or more specifically the science of the incredibly small, the mind-blowing and wonderfully exciting science of quantum physics.

CHAPTER 10

The Physics

Setting the Scene

Okay, so lots of people claim that they can travel outside of their body and they can 'perceive' things that cannot be perceived if they were not 'astrally travelling'. If this is really the case, then our present understanding of science is totally wrong.

If you speak to most professional scientists they will happily tell you that a belief in any form of out-of-body perception is totally contrary to what we know about modern science. Consciousness needs the brain in order to be, and to be outside of the brain is simply impossible.

Be that as it may, it is highly likely that such scientists will be specialists in the life sciences or the social sciences. The closer a scientist gets to the really hard sciences, such as physics and cosmology, the less sure they become. This is because they know that the latest research regarding the nature of the very small (subatomic 'particles') and the very large (galaxies) is not as black and white as we are led to believe.

I never cease to be surprised at how little the general public knows about quantum physics. It is as if there is some form of subtle conspiracy to keep a large majority of humanity blissfully unaware of the profound mysteries that particle physics has presented over the last hundred years or so. Indeed, I would go further and say that this majority's knowledge is based upon what was known 110 years ago and the last century of advances never happened.

Most people will know about Einstein and, if questioned, they may be aware that Einstein's theory of relativity is very difficult to understand. Some will add that Einstein showed that matter and energy are the same thing and that, at great speed, time itself dilates in some peculiar way. But that is about it. Most people know nothing about superposition, entanglement, quantum leaping, wave-particle duality and all the other intriguingly counterintuitive but regularly observed behaviours of subatomic 'wavicles'.

As a regular reader of such magazines as *New Scientist* and *Scientific American* I have made it my business to understand as best I can the implications of modern physics. Pick up any book in the popular science section of a bookshop and you will find serious (and not-so-serious) books written by some of the world's leading author-ities on this subject. These authors clearly show that they are both confused and excited by the implications of these new discoveries.

In order to appreciate exactly how odd things have become, how counterintuitive the real world is, we need to go back to basics. We need to understand exactly what physics is for.

From ancient times man has wanted to know what the world is made of. We see objects in space all around us. These objects seem solid and semi-permanent. But they must be made of smaller bits of 'something'. In around 400 BCE a Greek philosopher called Democritus suggested that everything, including space and time, is made up of tiny indestructible units. He called these units 'atoms' from the Greek word *atomos* – indivisible. But that was as far as he could go; humanity in those days had no way of proving or disproving such an idea. For the next 2,200 years this hypothesis was mostly forgotten until a schoolteacher called John Dalton was to resurrect the idea as a way of formulating a process by which matter can be manipulated. Applying some very practical principles, he discovered that all atoms of a given element were identical. He further suggested that, by combining two or more different kinds of atoms, chemical compounds could be formed. He carefully weighed his chemicals before and after they reacted with each other and, in doing so, calculated the ratios of different elements that went into well-known compounds. In this way he discovered a really reliable counting unit that could be applied to such things as steam pressure and the behaviour of gases.

Others carried forward these practical observations and by the end of the 19th century the 'atomic theory' had enabled scientists to predict the properties of all the commonly available chemical elements. Chemists were able to 'design' thousands of compounds that facilitated huge advances in industry and engineering.

While it was known how to manipulate this theory, there was no idea *how* it worked or *what*, indeed, these atoms were.

What was known, however, is that these atoms, in huge numbers, brought about the physical reality of all physical objects in the world and, by extrapolation, the universe itself. After the hugely significant discovery that each element had a different 'signature' when its light was broken down with a prism, astronomers were able to show that the visible universe was made up of the same elements found on Earth. By looking into space, scientists found new elements that were subsequently discovered here on Earth. Helium is an example. This element was first observed in 1868 when Pierre Janssen, a French astronomer, broke down the light coming from a solar eclipse and found a totally new spectral line signature.

Clearly, in order to bring about a solid object, atoms must, by pure logic, be solid themselves. The concept was of very small ball-like objects all crammed together in a solid mass. Indeed, this made sense. As you will know from your school days, water is a compound of hydrogen and oxygen and the smallest particle of water is, in fact, two atoms of hydrogen and one of oxygen. This compound particle is called a molecule, but a molecule is the smallest 'bit' that water can be. If the molecule is broken down it becomes hydrogen and oxygen. It was known for centuries that water had three forms – ice, liquid and steam. These states were related to temperature. When very cold, water is ice. As it is heated the molecules become agitated and move away from each other, allowing the flowing effect of water to be observed. When heated sufficiently to boiling point, the water changes to a gas. The molecules are no longer in contact with each other.

So it is obvious, big solid objects must be made up of trillions of much smaller, but still solid, objects. This is a totally logical assumption .... And it is totally wrong.

Everything you see around you, including this book, your body (and the brain doing the processing) is actually made up of trillions and trillions of bits of *empty space*! Solidity is an illusion brought about by some form of magic trick; even now, in the early 21st century, scientists struggle to explain how this process of something out of nothing takes place.

I can imagine that if you are encountering this fact for the first time, you will simply reject it as being totally ridiculous and illogical. May I ask that you sit back, maybe make yourself a coffee, and get ready to be amazed, because this, my dear reader, is the 'reality' of modern science. It is just that the scientists don't really like lay people knowing this, because it opens up more questions than they have answers to, at least not the kind of answers that Newton and Einstein would be happy with. Welcome to the two best-kept secrets of modern times – either reality is created by consciousness, or there are trillions of universes all containing versions of you and I.

The next few pages may be difficult to follow, but please bear with me. By the end you may be in a position to appreciate not only how all the ecsomatic experiences that we have discussed in this book may be explained scientifically within the present paradigm, but also how these experiences may be precursors to a new science in which mind is the prime element, not matter.

In order to have a basic understanding of these concepts one has to be introduced to another startling fact about how our confidence in the solidity and reality of the perceived universe, as presented by our senses, is an illusion. In simple terms, the oft quoted phrase 'seeing is believing' is utter nonsense. This can be shown by the discovery of electromagnetic fields and, from this, the electro-magnetic spectrum.

In his book *The Structure of Scientific Revolution* the American physicist Thomas Kuhn suggested that our scientific understanding of the world does not evolve gradually but in abrupt revolutions in which one scientific paradigm is replaced by another. The original paradigm was labelled 'Aristotelian' by Kuhn. This scientific world-view existed from the time of the ancient Greeks until Isaac Newton came along and swept it all away. The system proposed that the Earth was a non-moving object that the heavens revolved around in perfect circles. The natural state of all things was immobility and they could only move if they were pushed or acted upon by another object that was, itself, moving. All movement was started by the 'Prima Mobile', the First Mover, commonly known as God. In order for an object to move there had to be physical contact between the stationary object and that transferring motive power.

Newton came along in the 17th century and turned common sense on its head. He proved everything is in a state of movement unless it is stopped or slowed down in some way. Mobility is the natural state of all things. However, there was still a problem, and it was a simply observed phenomenon. Under certain circumstances objects seemed to be affected by other objects without any form of contact. One example of this is the force of gravity. As Newton himself supposedly observed, an apple falls to the ground. How does this happen? There is no physical contact and yet the apple moves through space from the tree to the ground; the apple is affected by a mysterious and totally invisible force. As we know, Newton's explanation was that this 'force field' was due to an attraction between the mass of the Earth and the mass of the apple. But this did not explain how the force actually worked. It was an earlier example of the 'spooky action at a distance' that was to disturb Einstein, 200 years later.

It was in April 1820 that an odd event in a laboratory at the University of Copenhagen was to precipitate a fundamental change in our understanding of the nature of the universe. Scientist Hans Christian Orsted was preparing for a lecture when he noticed that a compass needle was deflected from pointing to magnetic north when a nearby electric current from a battery was turned on and off. Magnetism and its ability to attract iron objects to it, without any physical contact, had long puzzled scientists and here was an apparent link between this and another mysterious physical property, electricity. Orsted's observation was not only to prove a relationship between electricity and magnetism, but also that a force field was involved in which there was no physical contact between the battery and the compass needle. Later, Michael Faraday was to suggest that electricity and magnetism were linked by something he termed the electromagnetic field. However, it was not until 1873 that James Clerk Maxwell proved that electricity and magnetism were the same thing, and also that the electromagnetic field was not simply local but universal. It existed everywhere. It was shown that modifications to this electromagnetic field travelled through space at the speed of light. This was a revolutionary insight. Suddenly space was not empty but contained a field that connected particles whether they were in contact or not.

The electromagnetic spectrum is, in effect, radiation. We perceive electromagnetic radiation as light and heat, but this is just a small part of the crucial component of the present scientific paradigm. Electromagnetic radiation travels in waves, and how the different types of radiation are perceived depends upon the 'wavelength' (the distance between each 'peak') and the 'frequency' (how many waves go past a certain point in a second). The shortest wavelengths with the greatest frequency are called gamma rays. The wavelength of a gamma ray is so tiny that each wave is the size of the nucleus inside an atom. Short wavelengths also mean that the wave can deliver more energy per unit of time. Indeed, heat, a form of energy, is simply another way in which elements of this spectrum are measured. Gamma rays are very hot, tens of millions of degrees centigrade. As the wavelength decreases so the amount of heat radiated also decreases. We move through X-rays (wavelength equal to an atom), ultraviolet light (wavelength equal to a molecule), visible light comes next (wavelength equal to a single-celled animal), then infrared (wavelength equal to a needle point), followed by microwaves (waves the size of a butterfly) and finally to radio waves that are many metres in wavelength. Only visible light, infrared and radio waves can actually penetrate the Earth's atmosphere and reach the surface.

Now, the fascinating thing about this electromagnetic spectrum is that the human eye can only see a very small section, the part we call 'visible light' for obvious reasons. Just how small this visible section is can be shown by an analogy. If the electromagnetic spectrum were a roll of movie film that stretched for 2,500 miles (this is the distance between London and Jerusalem), the visible spectrum would be the size of one film frame, about three inches. This is just how little we human beings see of the real universe that is out there and yet most of us believe that 'seeing is believing'! If we could see radio waves we would see a sky full of galaxies, not stars.

The discovery of the electromagnetic spectrum and many other scientific 'truths' led to a great feeling of smugness within the scientific community as the 20th century dawned. It was generally believed that humankind was very close to understanding all there was to know about physics. There were just a few equations that needed to be sorted out and that was it. However, there were one or two things that puzzled scientists. Most physicists ignored them, but one, Max Planck, found them worrying and, being a very conservative German scientist, he wanted answers.

The problem was with the electromagnetic spectrum. If energy came in a continual stream, then there were certain observed phenomena that could not be accounted for using this model. One was something called 'blackbody radiation'. There is not space to go into this in detail, but suffice to say that Planck and his associates were aware that the concept of radiation as a continual stream of energy was incompatible with recent measurements of blackbody radiation. In a moment of inspiration Planck was able to solve the mystery. The only way these anomalies could be explained was if radiation existed in little bursts or packets. He called these bursts 'quanta' after the Latin word for 'package'. Suddenly the maths worked. But there was more. Planck's new observation seemed to work for many other things as well, the most important being light itself. The logical conflict of light as a continuous wave with light as a particle carrying a precise amount of energy based upon its frequency, generated a new paradigm of science that, using Planck's term, became known as 'quantum physics'.

An integral part of quantum physics is the necessity for uncertainty to exist within our description of particle interactions. Newton's objective reality now had an uncertain statistical component added to it. In replacing the cosy world of Newtonian certitude (a place that many scientists, even now over 310 years later, never left) with quantum uncertainty, a huge chasm opened up between what the human mind could actually understand about nature and the evidence presented by repeated experimentation. Put simply, the world of the very small (the building blocks of everything around us, including our bodies and our brains) suddenly made no logical sense.

New theories have been proposed to account for these weird and wonderful observations. What we now have, at the start of the 21st century within mainstream physics, are three conflicting theories that dominate attempts to explain the universe. These are the Copenhagen Interpretation, the Many Worlds Interpretation and the Implicate Order. All three have their supporters and their detractors. But what is of more interest with regard to the subject of this book is that each one can be used to explain the OOB experience.

Surprised? Let me explain why, by systematically going through each alternative and showing how 'hard' science can explain the possibility of the ecsomatic experience as a real state.

The Copenhagen Interpretation

Although Planck's 'quanta' worked mathematically, he had not really explained why it was that certain curious effects took place. When light of a single frequency was shone onto thin metal foil, electrons were detected being knocked out of the surface. It was as if the light was hitting the surface and chipping the electrons off in the same way that a ball bearing would dislodge wood chips if thrown at high velocity at a plank of wood. This phenomenon, known as the 'photoelectric effect', made no sense. Light was known to be a wave; a disturbance in another medium, in the same way that a sound wave travels through air. The classic interpretation would be that the light waves acted like ocean waves hitting a pebble beach. As each wave comes in, it dislodges some pebbles. Therefore, it was logical to conclude that the more intense the illumination (i.e. brighter) the greater the energy delivered, so the more electrons dislodged. But no relationship was found when it was tested by German physicist Philip Lenard. Indeed, what was stranger was that there was a threshold at which no further electrons were ejected, no matter how bright the light. This was a real conundrum. But a solution was soon at hand.

In 1905 a young patent clerk by the name of Albert Einstein published a paper in the science journal *Annalen der Physik* that was to explain the photoelectric effect and advance Planck's quantum theory to another level. In simple terms, he suggested that light kicked out the electrons because light was not made up of waves but of tiny, solid particles called 'photons'. This may not seem that revolutionary, but ever since Isaac Newton had first discovered the wave nature of light, scientists had observed this to be the case. In 1801, English physicist Thomas Young showed that light flowed like a wave and since that time the wave properties of light were beyond any doubt. And yet here was this 26-year-old German suggesting otherwise, and proving it to be the case. In 1909 Einstein published a further paper suggesting that light had properties of duality, whereby under certain circumstances it is observed to behave as a wave, and under others as a particle. The question, then, was how could light be both a wave and a particle? In 1924 another young man was to shock even Einstein in his solution to this enigma. His name was Prince Louis de Broglie.

For his doctoral thesis de Broglie took Einstein's model of the photoelectric effect and suggested that the wave-duality of light extended to the entire physical world. For him this was not restricted to photons, but included the motion of a particle of any sort – photon, electron, proton or any other. Einstein was sent a copy of this paper and he was astounded. In his opinion de Broglie's hypothesis had 'lifted the great veil' and revealed a new understanding of how the physical universe really worked. In effect, de Broglie had suggested that all matter in the universe, from the smallest atom to the largest galaxy, has two aspects, a wave and a particle. The question was: what makes a particle decide to change from being a wave to being a particle?

The answer was so astounding that even today the vast majority of humanity has no idea that such a suggestion was ever posited, let alone subsequently proven time and time again. In my opinion, this is because the answer was so counterintuitive that it has simply been surreptitiously swept under the carpet. It is not exactly a secret, but it has not been shouted from the rooftops either. The reason is a simple one, because the answer states quite clearly that the act of observation makes the non-physical wave turn into a solid object! To be more precise, it is the availability of information created by a physical measurement that causes a non-physical probabilistic wave function to collapse into a physical particle.

In the mid 1920s some of the best brains in the world of physics gravitated to Copenhagen to work with the great physicist Niels Bohr. This group of scientists developed a model of the basic nature of matter that has now become known as the Copenhagen Interpretation. In 1926 two members of this group, Werner Heisenberg and Max Born, presented a paper proposing that the wave we have been discussing as a physical presence is not a wave in any normal sense that we can understand. For Born and Heisenberg it was a wave of 'probabilities'. This concept changed forever our understanding of the nature of reality. In the Born/Heisenberg model nothing exists until it is observed. Every particle has the 'probability' of being in one location or another. In effect, the particle is 'smeared out' across all possible locations. This is the wave filling all the possible space that the particle can be. When the particle is observed (what we mean by 'observed' I will return to later) the particle is forced to make a 'decision' as to where it should locate itself. In other words, there is a 'wave function', containing all the possible locations, that is 'collapsed' into a point location when it is observed or measured.

This theory is the most successful model of how the universe works that there has ever been. Every time it has been tested it has passed with flying colours. For many professional scientists this is the way the universe works. It may be totally illogical and counterintuitive, but that is the way it is. One of the most respected physicists of the late 20th century was Richard Feynman. Every year as he had the first intake of students for his particle physics lectures he would make the following statement:

> Do not keep saying to yourself, if you can possibly
> avoid it, 'But how can it be like that?' because you
> will get 'down the drain', into a blind alley from which
> nobody has yet escaped. Nobody knows how it can be
> like that.[56]

The major question that has kept scientists awake at night for the last 80 years is what is meant by an 'act of observation'? Some argue that it really means the act of measurement. For example, as soon as a measuring device comes into contact with the wave function, it collapses. Others have argued that the observer has to be a self-aware consciousness. In other words the observer has to be aware that they are observing something. A measuring device is not aware, only the person using the measuring device is.

The implications of this are absolutely astounding and central to my contention that ecsomatic states are real. In effect, the Copenhagen Interpretation suggests that *reality is created by an act of observation*. Without an observer there is no reality, just a void containing waves of probability waiting to be collapsed by a conscious mind. If this is the case, then each of us is creating our own version of reality as we look around. As you sit reading this book, what is behind you is probable rather than actual. By turning around and looking at it you turn that probability and its accompanying wave function into a physical reality.

The uncertainty associated with that probability is relatively small in the physical macro world and relatively large in the physical micro world; thus quantum effects are more noticeable when measuring small particles and missed altogether in everyday interactions.

This is exactly what Tom Campbell believes is happening in his physical matter reality (PMR) concept as presented in his *My Big Toe* books. Tom, you will recall, suggests that we perceive two levels of 'reality'. The first is the one we seemingly share with everybody else, consensual space for want of a better term. This is PMR. The second, termed non-physical matter reality, or NPMR, is the seemingly private inner world of dreams and ecsomatic experiences. Both are quasi-illusionary states, but both are objectively real in that they are generated by processes external to the mind. Indeed, both states are also pulled into existence by an 'act of observation', as Max Born suggested. The 'probability wave' of an object having the potential to be in one location rather than another is 'collapsed' when the observer's attention focuses on it. In the shared world of PMR, once an object has been 'collapsed', it remains in existence for all other observers, too.

Of course, the Copenhagen Interpretation is also uncannily similar to another ecsomatic state that we have discussed in some detail – lucid dreaming. You will recall that lucid dreaming is when the dreamer becomes aware that they are dreaming. As soon as this happens they are able, to a greater or lesser extent, to manipulate their dream environment. However, expert lucid dreamers, such as Robert Waggoner and Ian Wilson, regularly point out that in an LD state the dreamscape is rendered while it is being observed.

Nevertheless, the sensation of lucid dreaming is considered by many to be quite different to other ecsomatic experiences such as remote viewing and out-of-body experiences. For these to be real there has to be a way in which the mind can immediately locate its perception facilities in another place, as in the case of remote viewing, or, as in the case of OBEs, actually travel to another place. Interestingly, both these states can be explained by applying two more aspects of modern quantum theory; these are the Many-Worlds Interpretation (MWI) or Many-Minds Interpretation and the mysterious phenomenon known as Non-Locality. I wish to discuss Non-Locality first and then move on to the fascinating MWI.

Non-Locality

The mystery all started, back in 1935, when Albert Einstein was desperately trying to disprove what, in his mind, were the counter-intuitive implications of the 'new' physics discussed in the section above. We have seen how this proposed that the act of observa-tion by a conscious mind made subatomic particles change from a 'wave of probable states' to an actual point-state that was physically measurable. This was totally illogical as far as Einstein was concerned. It suggested that things simply did not exist if we were not looking at them. He once famously stated that he simply could not believe that the moon was not there if he was not looking at it. In the opinion of Einstein there had to be a deeper level of observed reality in which common sense again prevailed. This was to become known as the 'hidden variables'.

In 1935 Einstein got together with two associates, Nathan Rosen and Boris Podolsky, and proposed a 'thought experiment' that would highlight just how logically flawed this idea of 'observer-based' reality was.

In a paper that was published later that year, Einstein and his two associates asked a simple question: what would happen if a particle decayed, sending two protons off in opposite directions in order to conserve momentum?

Imagine that the two protons are a pair of red snooker balls, in some way attached to each other. Another snooker ball is propelled at them, causing them to fly off in different directions. This is analogous to the instant decaying of a particle (the original linked balls). As they fly apart, each carries a type of imprint of the other in the form of angular momentum. One spins in one direction, the other in the opposite direction. One will have what is called 'up' spin and the other will have 'down' spin. Now, until the particles are 'observed' by an act of measurement there is no way of telling which one has which angle of spin. But, once one is observed to have one type of spin, it is easy to know the spin of the other ball. If the observed ball has 'up' spin then the other must have 'down' spin. I always find this easier to explain by using colours. Imagine that the impact of the cue ball makes two 'entangled' red balls change colour, one becomes green and the other becomes blue. These are the only two possible colours. Now, because the impact is so fast we cannot see which ball goes in which direction. Let us further assume that the person hitting the balls is a professional snooker player who pockets both balls in different parts of the table. We go to one pocket and see that it contains a blue snooker ball. We instantly know from this that, logically, in one of the other pockets will be a green ball. There is nothing weird about this in any way, but in the world of quantum physics this is one of the weirdest things known to modern science. Let me explain.

According to the Copenhagen Interpretation, after the moment of impact the two balls, as they are not 'observed', enter a peculiar state in which they both have the 'potential' to be blue or green. This is technically known as 'superposition', a concept we will encounter later. Remember that the random choice of being either colour takes place *after* the impact of the cue ball; beforehand they are both red. They both have a statistical potential of 50/50 of being blue and a 50/50 chance of being green. In this unobserved state the two balls travel across the snooker table and enter their respective pockets. The 'observer' then checks one pocket and in doing so 'collapses the wave potential (known as its "function")' of the observed ball and forces it to decide to be blue or green. Are you with me so far? Okay then; as soon as the observer forces the collapse of the wave of the first ball and sees a green ball, a 'message' is sent to the second ball telling it that it too must collapse its wave function into a solid blue ball.

Using different terminology this is exactly what Einstein and his two associates suggested would happen if the Copenhagen Interpretation was correct. Einstein pointed out that the signal carrying the message would cross the space between the two pockets instantaneously to change the second ball from a *potential* green or blue ball to an *actual* blue ball. He called this 'spooky action at a distance'. He further pointed out that it violated the cast-iron physical law that nothing, not even a message, can travel faster than the speed of light, and as the message travels instantly from one pocket to another, it is travelling many, many, factors faster than light speed. Indeed, its speed could be considered infinite.

As far as Einstein was concerned, this thought experiment, known to posterity as the EPR Paradox after the initials of its creators, showed how ridiculous Bohr's theory was. It was self-evident, stated Einstein, that the two particles had been in existence at all times of their journeys and had had their individual properties (spin or colour) from the moment of departure. There was no spooky action at a distance; just a straightforward, logical proposition that if one is observed to be green then the other is blue, and has been blue since the moment of impact with the other ball.

It is highly likely that the reader whose mindset is firmly placed in practical, Newtonian physics will agree with Einstein and his associates; any contrary position is clearly ridiculous.

Modern physics has shown that Einstein was wrong and Bohr's illogical Copenhagen Interpretation was right, at least as far as 'spooky action at a distance' goes. It has been shown by experimentation that particles do, in fact, communicate instantaneously and in doing so, call into question some of the basic tenets of physics; that faster-than-light communication is possible, or, that relationship between mind and matter is far stranger than we could ever have imagined.

For nearly 30 years EPR stood as a logical proof that, although Bohr's physics may have worked in practice, there was something very wrong about his Copenhagen Interpretation and its suggestion that matter needed 'an act of observation' to come into existence. However, in 1964 an Irish mathematician published a paper in a scientific journal that was to shake modern science to its core. So revolutionary was this paper, and the real-life experiments that it subsequently engendered, that traditional physicists still try to ignore the implications and hope that embarrassing truths will simply go away; a surprisingly large percentage of well-educated people remain totally unaware of them.

The mathematician in question was Dr John Bell and the paper was entitled 'Can Quantum Mechanical Description of Physical Reality Be Considered Complete?' So what did Bell's paper suggest that was so revolutionary?

EPR could not really challenge the Copenhagen Interpretation because no experiment could be set up to test its conclusions. Bell decided to take a different approach. He supposed that Einstein was right and that objects in our world do have physically real properties and do not need the act of observation to bring them into being; a proposition that most individuals who are unaware of the mysteries of quantum physics would wholeheartedly agree with. He then further supposed that when two objects are separated from each other in space, then what happens to one should have no effect upon the other. The former statement can be termed 'reality' and the latter 'separability'. In order for quantum theory, as suggested by the Copenhagen Interpretation, to be right these observable quantities must be unequal, one must be larger than the other. This was termed Bell's Inequality.

In effect Bell's paper proved that what quantum theory predicted was correct and that his and Einstein's predictions were wrong; 'Spooky action at a distance' does take place.[57] But this was purely a hypothetical model. What was needed was a real-life experiment that would prove the inequality to be more than a nice theory. This took place in 1982 in Paris when French physicist Alain Aspect and a group of associates at the Institut d'Optique in Orsay near Paris conducted a real-life version of EPR and found that Bell's hypothesis was correct.[58] Once two particles are linked together, or *entangled*, one will immediately react if something is done to the other.

In 1998 another series of tests at the University of Geneva demonstrated the non-local entanglement of photons over 11km of optical fibre. In 2004 the same team extended this distance to over 50km.[59]

What this proves is earth-shattering in its implications. It means that at a deeper level of reality than we are aware of, *everything* is linked to everything else. Separability is an illusion. Everything is part of one huge *something* in which communication is instantaneous, however far apart the individual components are.

So what does this mean with regard to the OOB state? Some physicists believe that entanglement does away with the whole idea that objects exist in space – that they are 'local'. Bell's Inequality, along with the results of Aspect's experiment, suggests that objects are 'non-local' in that they are, in some very profound way, part of the same thing. By this I mean that the two 'entangled' particles may 'know' the state of each other not because they are communicating in some 'spooky action at a distance' way but because they are, in fact *the same object*. This is not such a weird idea as it first appears; Richard Feynman once suggested that the whole universe may consist of one electron moving at infinite speed. If that is the case, then entanglement is the natural state of the universe.

When applied to ecsomatic states, entanglement is a perfect explanation. The question of how a person can perceive information miles away from the location their body (soma) is easily answered because separateness is, as Bell has shown, an illusion. Everything is entangled and all information is available at all locations within the universe. As we saw in an earlier chapter, Ingo Swann claimed that he distance-viewed the surface of Jupiter. As distance is simply another term for separation it is clear that such a thing could happen.

However, entanglement fails to explain one of the real mysteries of ecsomatic perception: why is it that credible individuals such as Ingo Swann, Robert Monroe and others, consistently fail to prove their abilities under laboratory conditions? Why is it that Ingo identified mountains on Jupiter when it is known that no such structures exist? Is it simply that they are pretending they have these skills? Spending any time with individuals who claim to have had ecsomatic experiences, or have distance-viewed places and people, brings one to the conclusion that these people are really experiencing a genuine altered state. So why do they get things so wrong?

For me the clue lies in Robert Monroe's reports of his travels to Locale 3. I think that the astral travellers do, indeed, go somewhere else, but this somewhere else is not in the external universe, as we understand it to be. I am suggesting that the answer to this puzzle can be explained without recourse to any 'New Age' waffle through a new model that applies two simply amazing, but seemingly conflicting, modern theories about the real nature of the universe, consciousness and reality, to the ecsomatic experience. These are called the Implicate Order of Professor David Bohm and the mind-blowing Many Worlds Interpretation of Dr Hugh Everett III. If you have never encountered these theories before, I guarantee that after reading the next few pages your view of the universe and your understanding of your role within it will be permanently changed.

The Implicate Order

Non-locality suggests that when two quantum systems have interacted, their wave functions become what is known as 'phase-entangled'. This means that once one of the entangled wave functions is collapsed, the other one does so immediately, however great the distance between the two systems. As we have seen, this is Einstein's 'spooky action at a distance'. It implies that by sharing a wave function, the two systems, in effect, become the same system. This is not restricted to single pairs of wave systems; the number of wave systems involved is limitless. Now this suggests something really amazing. In the first milliseconds of the Big Bang, all matter came into existence from what is known as a 'singularity'. Everything that exists, every electron, photon and every other subatomic particle, was 'created' at that moment. Everything we observe (and probably all that we cannot observe such as 'dark energy' and 'dark matter') is derived from these initial particles which were part of this singularity. It is reasonable to conclude that all these particles became 'phase entangled' during these first nanoseconds and then, like the two particles in the Aspect experiment, these countless particles shot off in various directions and began to build matter – all matter. So, in effect, this means that everything in the universe is entangled – you, me, the book in your hand, the planet Jupiter and the Andromeda Galaxy – we are all part of each other.

But it gets even stranger if we apply the theories of particle physicist David Bohm to this stunning observation. Professor Bohm was a great supporter of Einstein. He believed that the Copenhagen Interpretation was, as Einstein suggested, incomplete.

Bohm found himself agreeing with Einstein that there must be some form of reality underneath the seemingly random behaviour of particles. In the same way that the swirls and eddies of a swollen river seem random in their movement when viewed from a bridge, those same random swirls are joined together as part of the flow beneath the surface. Bohm wanted to look below the 'surface' of quantum behaviour, find the 'hidden variables', as he termed them, and show that classical mechanics remain consistent.

He faced one huge obstacle, however; a mathematical formula called the 'Von Neumann Proof'. This first appeared in 1931 and it seemed that the model of reality, as presented by the Copenhagen Interpretation, was where everything stopped. Science need not delve any further because there was no further to go. In order to get to his 'hidden variables', Bohm had to disprove the famed equation. In 1952 he did just that. He uprooted this 'proof' by constructing a model of the electron with classical attributes whose behaviour matched the predictions of the quantum theory. In this model, the electron is viewed as an ordinary particle, with one key difference: the electron has access to information about its environment.

The way in which the particle communicates with the rest of its environment Bohm termed the 'quantum potential'. It is through this that all the seemingly strange at-a-distance communications implied by EPR, and proven by Aspect, take place. Rather like two waves may seem like individual towers of water, if you look below you will see that the ocean links them. So how 'low' do we need to look to find the 'ocean surface' for our quantum waves?

For Bohm the 'where the hidden variables sit' is to be found between the smallest distance that science can detect and the smallest possible distance that physics can allow. When this is first encountered it is an extremely strange concept, but it seems that at a distance of 10^{-33}cm it is impossible to have any space. Bohm argued that the smallest distance that physics can detect is 10^{-17}cm. This leaves an unknown realm that spans 16 orders of magnitude in relative size, which is comparable to the size difference between our ordinary macroscopic world and the smallest detectable physical distance (10^{-17}cm). It is within this realm that the 'quantum potential' functions. As this empty space exists at such a minute size, it cannot possibly contain anything; it is, in effect, a vacuum. But as we shall discover later, this vacuum is far from empty. At this point please consider the fact that this vast area of empty space is everywhere around you and also inside of you. Most significantly, as we shall also discover later, this vast emptiness exists within and between every single neuron of your brain.

Bohm's 'quantum potential' is a wave-like information system that guides the electron via the medium of the 'hidden variable'. He uses the analogy of an aircraft guidance system in support of his theory. Aircraft change course in response to radio-wave instructions. However, the radio wave does not provide the power to change course, purely the active information. It is the airliner itself that supplies the energy to make the required course revisions. In the same way the quantum potential instructs the electron to make certain changes to its condition.

In Bohm's concept of quantum mechanics, all particles are linked by this quantum potential within a huge interconnected web. Rather like a spider can tell movement anywhere within its web, so is it for the particles in the quantum potential. This is the way the particles communicate in the Aspect experiment. According to Bohm, relativity is not violated because it simply does not function at the deeper level where the quantum potential exerts its influence.

So how can we visualize the way these hidden variables act? Bohm came up with an ingenious way of showing how observers, without all the information at hand, can confuse what they see and make totally wrong assumptions. He asked us to imagine creatures living on another planet. These creatures have never seen fish and have no concept of what an aquarium is. As we cannot send them an aquarium or fish, a solution is to set up two closed-circuit TV cameras pointing at real fish swimming in an aquarium. One camera is directed at the aquarium's front and one at its side. Our alien friends rig up two television sets, one to receive the signal from one camera and one to receive the signal from the other. Not knowing any better, the aliens quite rightly assume that they are looking at two separate entities, not one fish. After a time our clever aliens note that there seems to be a definite relationship between the two entities. Although they do not move in the same direction or look exactly alike at any one time, they do show similarities; when one faces the front, the other faces the side, for example. The aliens come to the conclusion that some form of subliminal, but instantaneous, communication is taking place. But this is not the case. The two fish are actually one and the same.

This, says Bohm, is precisely what is going on between the subatomic particles in Aspect's experiment. The apparently instantaneous transfer of information between subatomic particles is really telling us that there is a deeper level of reality we are not privy to; a more complex dimension beyond our own that is analogous to the aquarium. And, he adds, we view objects such as subatomic particles as separate from one another because we are seeing only a portion of their reality.

Bohm suspected that everything is, in some way, contained by and contains everything else. In other words everything is, as he termed it 'enfolded' upon itself. What we see as separate objects are linked at a much lower level of reality. Just like the fish in the aquarium analogy, where a single entity was perceived as two entities because of the perceptual tools available to the observers, so it is with our universe. The two particles in the Aspect experiment communicate at a distance because they are enfolded in each other. That is how the communication takes place. In Bohm's view, underlying our perception of separate things is an underlying order of wholeness. This enfolding involves everything that exists, including human consciousness itself. Bohm said:

> In the implicate order the totality of existence is
> enfolded within each region of space (and time). So,
> whatever part, element, or aspect we may abstract in
> thought, this still enfolds the whole and is therefore
> intrinsically related to the totality from which it has
> been abstracted. Thus, wholeness permeates all that is
> being discussed, from the very outset.[60]

Bohm was fortunate in that there is one modern invention that implies every part of the greater object contains versions of itself. This invention is the hologram. Holograms, so much taken for granted these days, are very peculiar things. Laser light is split into two beams, one of which is reflected off the object to be recorded. This beam arrives at a photographic plate where it interferes with the first beam. To the naked eye the pattern on the photographic plate is seen as simply meaningless swirls and patterns. However, when this plate is illuminated with laser light, an amazing effect takes place; the swirls give forth a three-dimensional image of the original object. This image can be viewed from any angle. The photographic plate contains a hidden, or enfolded, order. This is well known. What is less well known is that if a holographic film is cut into pieces and again illuminated with laser light, each piece does not, as one would expect, hold a part of the full image, but has a miniature copy of the whole original image. This is slightly fuzzy, but nevertheless can be identified as such. This peculiar effect vindicates, in a very visible way, Bohm's idea that the part contains the whole. The form and structure of the entire object is encoded within each region of the photographic record.

From this, Bohm suggested that the whole universe can be thought of as a kind of giant, flowing hologram, or holomovement, in which a total order is contained, in some implicit sense, in each region of space and time. The explicate order is a projection from higher dimensional levels of reality, and the apparent stability and solidity of the objects and entities composing it are generated and sustained by a ceaseless process of enfoldment and unfoldment, for subatomic particles are constantly dissolving into the implicate order and then reforming or re-emerging.

In recent years, interest in the ideas and theories of David Bohm has shown a huge resurgence. In November 2009 I attended a symposium in London in which a group of physicists presented papers on the explanatory power of Bohm's work. As we understand more and more about the nature of the subatomic universe, so it is that Bohm's star continues to rise for those not constrained by the straitjacket of the present scientific paradigm. I suspect that the results of the experiments taking place at the Large Hadron Collider (LHR) on the Swiss-French border may yet prove Bohm to be correct.

If David Bohm's concept of enfoldment is a reasonable alternative to 'spooky action at a distance', then we have another possible explanation for the ecsomatic state. Indeed, by extrapolation, we also have an explanation for telepathy, remote viewing, past-life memories, precognition and possibly even ghosts. Just as every portion of a hologram contains the image of a whole, so it is with the universe. Every portion is enfolded into the whole. This means that, if we knew how to find it, we could see the Andromeda Galaxy floating in the liquid that surrounds our eye. Also within that eye will be found every historical event that has ever happened; Napoleon is still retreating from Moscow and Neil Armstrong is still making his 'one small step for man' on the surface of the Moon.

But this idea becomes even odder. Each enfoldment will contain other enfoldments. For example, each of us will carry, in each atom of our body, images of our own past and our own future disappearing into the distance, like the images on two mirrors reflecting each other to eternity.

In Bohm's model such phenomena as remote viewing, lucid dreaming and out-of-the-body experiences are totally explicable, even natural. If everything is linked to everything else, then consciousness is not constrained to the brain but can travel within its own 'inner space', which, in turn, contains the whole universe. This really solves the problem of whether or not the brain creates consciousness, because they are both aspects of the same thing. That Ingo Swann could 'see' the surface of Io whilst lying in a bed in the United States is completely understandable. He didn't travel out into the space outside his brain, but travelled inward into the depths of his own subconscious and there he found another location, as real as the one millions of miles away in space.

Of course, this does not really explain how it is that highly effective distance viewers, such as Ingo Swann, Robert Monroe and many others, seem to fail when asked to prove their skills in laboratory conditions or appear to perceive incorrect data when they 'travel' within Monroe's 'Locale 1'. Also, Bohm's theory does not explain Monroe's other two Locales that suggest very different environments from those existing on Earth and possibly anywhere else within our consensual universe. For example, how can we explain Monroe's encounter with 'I There'? Could it be that certain ecsomatic experiences involve travelling to alternate universes that may be outside of this universe? My answer to this is yes and I believe that the theory of an eccentric physicist by the name of Hugh Everett III contains the answer to this second major mystery of ecsomatic states.

The Many-Worlds Interpretation

In a famous demonstration to show how illogical the observer-generated wave-function collapse was, physicist Irwin Schrödinger had proposed a thought experiment. He suggested that a cat be placed inside a sealed box with no windows. Also inside this box is a bottle of deadly gas, and poised above the box is a small hammer being held back by a latch. In turn, the latch is connected to a detector. This detector is programmed to scan a piece of radioactive material for the decay of one particular atom, an event that is known to have a 50/50 probability of taking place. If the atom *does* decay, the detector will send a signal to the latch instructing it to release the hammer. Like a latter-day feline equivalent of the 'Sword of Damocles', the hammer falls upon the bottle, smashing it and thus releasing the poisonous gas. Obviously this will result in the immediate death of the poor cat. Conversely, if no decay takes place then the hammer does not fall and the cat continues to live. We cannot confirm the state of the cat until we open the box and look inside. According to Bohr and his associates, the wave function needs an observer to facilitate its collapse, which in turn will bring about the decay or non-decay of the atom in question. Thus, until observed, the cat is in a curious alive-and-dead situation. As far as Schrödinger was concerned, his mind experiment proved that the 'statistical interpretation' was simply illogical.

The followers of the Copenhagen Interpretation stuck to their guns. They suggested that the cat was, indeed, in a 'hybrid' state of neither alive nor dead until the box was opened and the act of observation caused all the statistical possibilities to collapse into one observed state: a dead cat or a very alive one.

In 1957 the young Hugh Everett completed his PhD thesis. In this he proposed a radical, and totally new, solution to the problem of the observer-induced collapse of the wave function. This problem was the lack of seemingly commonsense logic that underpinned the Copenhagen Interpretation.

Like many others Everett simply could not accept such an illogical position, but the problem was that the Copenhagen interpretation worked – all the predictions made when it was applied to observed phenomena proved correct. While Everett accepted the validity of the model, he proposed a different interpretation.

For him it was logically nonsensical to believe that the wave function was only brought into existence by observation of a conscious mind. Of course the wave existed before observation and it continued after. It simply changed. So how did his new, rational and non-paranormal, proposal explain what takes place?

Everett suggested that the wave function itself splits into two realities: one where it collapses after the atomic decay and one where it doesn't. In effect, both realities exist together. When the box is opened, the observer in turn splits into two identical versions of himself, one of whom observes the cat dead and one who observes the cat alive. In this way Everett solved the horrible idea that mind was in some way different to matter.

What a solution! Instead of having a consciousness bringing material reality into existence, we have a science-fiction scenario of parallel universes. Thus, if one accepts Everett's proposal, one version of the scientist goes off and writes up one report, whereas in the other universe the other version writes a different report. Very rapidly a ripple of cause and effect changes each universe, initially in a small way, but as each new scenario engenders its own outcome, so the two mirror universes diverge into potentially very different places.

Everett's proposal, known now as the Many-Worlds Interpretation (MWI), does not stop there. The actual bifurcation of the universe took place not at the point of observation, but at the point of the quantum event; the 'decision' made by the atom to decay or not. That event will have caused its own alternative scenarios at the quantum level, causing split compounded upon split. Indeed Everett, and his later champion Bryce DeWitt, suggest that the universe splits at every quantum event and each new universe begins splitting in turn – and it has been doing this since the first millisecond of the Big Bang!

Thus, taken to its logical conclusion, the Many-Worlds Interpretation implies that all possible scenarios have happened or will happen in this new, rapidly inflating multiverse.

In the late 1980s a survey of 72 of the world's leading cosmologists came up with the following responses as regards MWI:

- 58 per cent said that they believed Everett's theory was true
- 18 per cent said that they did not accept it
- 13 per cent replied that they thought it was possible but had yet to be convinced
- the remaining 11 per cent had no opinion either way

Among those who agreed were such illustrious names as Stephen Hawking and Nobel Laureates Murray Gell-Mann and Richard Feynman. Gell-Mann and Hawking recorded reservations with the name 'Many-Worlds', but not with the theory's content. Nobel Laureate Steven Weinberg is also mentioned as a Many-Worlder. In a wider context Gell-Mann has described himself as an adherent to the post-Everett interpretation.

In practical terms what the Many-Worlds Interpretation suggests is that there are literally trillions upon trillions of universes, and these universes are all splitting continually into more and more universes. It is reasonable to conclude that to all intents and purposes the number of universes might as well be infinite. As we have already discovered, this splitting has been going on since the first microseconds of the Big Bang.

This means that every possible outcome of every event will happen in one or more universes. In turn, this means that every possible event that can take place will, or has already, taken place somewhere within this rapidly inflating 'macroverse'. You and I, and every other living being, are part of this inflation; there is a version of you that has lived every possible outcome of every possible decision you made, from the moment of your birth to the moment of your death. But it becomes more complex because you do not live your life in isolation. Your parents also will have made myriads of decisions, as will their parents in turn, right back through your ancestry. Some of these decisions may have involved moving to other places in the world. In fact, logic demands that they will have decided to live in every habitable location on the Earth. There will be versions of you born in every village and town in your own country, plus similar versions in every village in Burma, Peru, Norway and every other country on the planet. Some versions of you will have radically different cultural backgrounds and world-views, whereas others will be virtually identical – with every gradation between also represented in this wonderful macroverse.

The really interesting conundrum is that in some universes you may even be a different person. Your parents may have not made love at the moment you should have been conceived. If they delayed five minutes would that baby still be you or would it be another individual? The possibilities are endless, but one thing is clear – this makes your life, and all your potential lives, far more complex than you could ever have dreamed.

So let us imagine for a second that Everett and Bohm are both right – after all they both suggest theories opposing the idea that consciousness collapses the wave function – if this is the case then there are countless versions of you living countless variations of your life and they are all *enfolded* within you. Could this explain why sometimes we visit strange places in our dreams? Is this why lucid dreamers encounter strange worlds and locations? Could it be that all these places and locations are both out there and enfolded within us all?

Recent suggestions by Professor Stephen Hawking and an associate, Thomas Hertog of CERN, make this an even more fascinating proposition. They have presented a complex mathematical model proposing something that they term the 'observer created universe'. They argue that all these universes do not branch off and exist in isolation, but they exist simultaneously in a state of 'superposition'. You will recall that this is the state a particle is in before it is 'observed'. It exists in a superposition of all possible locations where it may statistically be found when the probability wave collapses. Amazingly, Hawking and Hertog suggest that all the trillions of universes are out there waiting for each of us to make a decision. When we do so, the 'wave function' of the universe that contains the outcome of that decision collapses, leaving all the other potential universes to continue in a state of superposition with all the others.

Let us step back and take account of exactly what one of the world's leading physicists is suggesting – you are creating your own universe as you go along, and so is every other consciousness. And this goes for all the other people you interact with in a lifetime. We are all existing in our own personal computer game in which each decision brings about a different version of reality, but (and this is very important to grasp) the *potential outcome* of each decision exists whether or not you choose it.

It would certainly explain why Robert Monroe was able to meld his mind into that of his 'I There' associate in Locale 3, and at the same time it could explain why some of Monroe's 'out-of-body' perceptions in Locale 1 were slightly different to how they actually were when he checked them out. Maybe Dr Bradshaw did speak to him in one universe, but not in another.

But this is all supposition on my part. In order to present this as a possibility rather than simply an amusing proposition, I need to present hard evidence from the leading edge of scientific thought that such an idea is not as crazy as it sounds. If the universe is entangled in some way, and consciousness is somehow the 'creator' of matter, how does this work? It is one thing proving, as Blake once said, that heaven exists in a wild flower, but quite another to present it as a potential *fact*.

ORCH-OR

Fact it may well prove to be, if British theoretical physicist Professor Roger Penrose and American anaesthesiologist Professor Stuart Hamerhoff have anything to do with it. If their suggestions are correct, then the weird and wonderful world of entangled particles and collapsed wave functions all exist for one reason and one reason alone – to facilitate consciousness and allow that consciousness to experience Everett's macroverse in all its glory.

These much-criticized pioneers have been working on a model that suggests the borderline between the microcosmic universe of quantum weirdness and the safe, deterministic universe of Newtonian physics can be found within the deep structures of the human brain. This is where quantum insanity turns into Newtonian sanity. They call this process Orchestrated Objective Reduction or ORCH-OR.

In order to appreciate the power of this concept we need to understand another – something called quantum coherence.

Quantum coherence is exhibited when large numbers of particles cooperate collectively in a single state. For example, the intense narrow beam of a laser is a perfect example. In this state all the light photons lack individual identities. They have become *coherent*. When stimulated in a specific way, all the photons collectively move to a higher energy state that is identical for all of them. This is a non-linear phase transition, meaning that it suddenly happens to all of them at the same moment. This is what makes laser light different to ordinary light, which is *in*coherent. Technically, this collective state is known as a *Bose-Einstein condensate* and many consider this to be a completely new form of matter. What is particularly significant about these B-E condensates is that they can be observed by the naked eye.

In order for the B-E condensates to form, there must be non-local communication between the particles. As we have seen from our discussion involving Bell's Inequality and the Aspect experiment, such states involve instantaneous communication of information between all the elements. It is as if each part is an element of a whole that 'knows' instantly about the state of all the other elements.

What is more amazing is that these peculiar B-E condensates have been found to exist within the human body. Indeed, it has been discovered that much of all living things is *liquid crystalline* in structure. For example, the collagen in bone is a semi-solid substance and is referred to as 'liquid crystal'. If you have ever used a pocket calculator you will have seen liquid crystals in action. But it is an extremely odd state of matter, neither liquid nor solid but a peculiar hybrid state. It is now known that information is transferred instantaneously within this state. Nearly all the connecting tissues and cell membranes contain this substance. Possibly of great significance, within all the cells of the body can be found tiny structures that are, in effect, biological Bose-Einstein condensates. Called microtubules, these self-organizing tubular protein structures may hold the secret of ecsomatic experiences and remote viewing, maybe even a channel by which we can all visit other dimensions, and, most amazingly, they may even explain consciousness itself.

These intriguing structures can be found in all cells of the body that have a nucleus. They are responsible for communication across each cell and, as such, have been called the cell's 'brain'. As the name implies, microtubules are both microscopic and tubular in shape. In some brain cells (neurons) they can be surprisingly long, some reaching nearly a metre in length, and bundled in arrangements consisting of hundreds or even thousands of individual structures. These bundled structures are reminiscent of fibre optics and indeed they have a great similarity with this man-made form of communication because they function in a similar way in that they send information using a form of light propagation. Significantly, it has been shown that the coherent single-photon micropulses of light that are sent along the length of each individual microtubule are generated from Bose-Einstein condensation. In other words, the communication processes that the microtubules use is also facilitated by quantum effects.

It was the peculiar computer-like nature of microtubules that first caught the attention of Professor Stuart Hamerhoff of the University of Arizona Medical School. As an anaesthesiologist, Hamerhoff had long been fascinated by exactly what was taking place when a person was placed under general anaesthetic – that is, when rendered totally unconscious. It was, for him, as if the drugs literally took away consciousness during the time of their effectiveness. With the exception of the loss of consciousness, the brain continues functioning as it always does. However, being in such an anaesthetic state is not the same as a deep sleep as many people believe. There is no dreaming and absolutely no sensation of pain. Of course, if there is no consciousness within the brain at this time then there is nothing to feel the pain. This is of profound philosophical importance. Where does consciousness go at this time? Is it simply 'switched off' in a state akin to death? Or is it simply that the anaesthetics stop communication between consciousness and the body?

Now it may come as some surprise to you, as it did for me in researching this section, that although physicians know the effects of general anaesthetics, they do not have a real idea *why* they work or indeed *how* they work. This is still an area of pure theory with new suggestions being presented from time to time in the medical journals. Could this be because the researchers are working within the wrong paradigm? As long as they continue to pursue the materialistic-deterministic model, they are doomed to failure because they are looking for the answers in the wrong places.

It seems that Stuart Hamerhoff is not making this mistake. As an eclectic and broad-minded thinker, he was keen to apply the latest findings of quantum physics to this mystery. He was intrigued by the role of microtubules in this process. Not restricting himself to the idea that consciousness is some form of illusion, he worked on the model that this ephemeral state of self-awareness was being blocked in some way by the anaesthetics. He knew from his training that the drugs specifically targeted the microtubules and, from this, concluded that the microtubules had a crucial role in the generation of consciousness.

At a similar time, British theoretical physicist Roger Penrose had written a book called *The Emperor's New Mind,* pointing out that the human brain would have to be far more complex than was possible if it functioned in a similar way to a super-computer. He suggested a solution could be found in applying quantum physics to the way the brain collects and processes information. Professor Hamerhoff read this book, contacted Professor Penrose, and suggested that maybe they should work together in developing a joint theory as to how consciousness may arise within the deep structures of the brain.

Penrose and Hamerhoff now propose a working model of how the wave function may be collapsed into a point particle within the microtubules themselves. In other words, Stuart and Roger make the amazing case that these tiny structures create 'reality' by forcing a wave of probabilities into a physical object that has mass and location. This is an incredible idea that has far-reaching implications for our understanding of the universe. If correct, it means that mind really does create matter not the other way round.

The implication is that every self-aware being is accessing information not from the external 'phenomenal' world but from the inner universe of quantum superposition and Bohm's model, now known as the 'implicate order'. If this is the case then our model of the phenomenal world is created internally, and then projected outwards to create the illusion of a real place located in space and time, both of which are mysteries for the present scientific paradigm. In this way the weird behaviour of particles coming into existence by the act of observation can be explained. It is a completely self-referential and fully enclosed feedback-loop.

Indeed, to state that consciousness exists or does not exist in the brain is to miss the point altogether. It exists everywhere as part of Bohm's 'implicate order'. It is enfolded within the universe itself and contains the universe within itself. Furthermore, this would mean that consciousness has access to all the information available within this matrix. Could this be a model for a new science that can explain the ecsomatic experience?

CHAPTER 11

The 'Intrasomatic' Experience

The Problem

Before I embarked upon this book I had no hard-and-fast opinions about the ecsomatic experience. As I began my review of the evidence for veridical proof, I was both surprised and disappointed that I found very little, if any, proving that individuals could, by force of will, leave their body and view information elsewhere and unavailable to everyday perception. All of the classic cases that are, time after time, cited as 'proof' of ecsomatic perceptions in book after book, sadly fell apart when looked at in any detail.

However, as soon as I started looking into the science, I found that such out-of-body perceptions may be available under certain neurochemical conditions or brain-stimulated altered states of consciousness.

So here was the mystery. The empirical evidence for subjective out-of-body perceptions was simply not there, but these people clearly were experiencing something out of the ordinary. I cannot simply believe that they were all liars and charlatans. What did Robert Monroe have to gain by writing his first book? He was a successful businessman. Indeed, in the preface to the second edition of *Journeys Out of the Body* he describes his personal concerns about how the book would be received by his business associates. His career could have easily been destroyed had it not been the case that many others had experienced similar things, but were frightened to talk about them for fear of ridicule. Ingo Swann was clearly seeing places and locations in his semi-sleep state; these were real to him. As I have said, I too have had these experiences and I know that the places that are 'seen' during these hypnopompic or hypnagogic states look and feel very real. They contain an inner logic to their structure that is totally convincing.

If the statistical research is to be believed, this phenomenon is extremely common. According to a study made in 1984 by Glackenberg and LaBerge, roughly one out of every five people will undergo an OBE at some time during his or her lifetime. In the UK alone this suggests *at least* 20 million OOB experiences over an average period of 70 years. This is 285,714 a year, 5,495 a week or 784 *every single day* ... and yet, there no convincing veridical case available to prove the reality of the phenomenon.

I have to accept that, without access to the original documents, some of Swann's distance perceptions were surprisingly accurate. His drawings and maps of distance-viewed locations are amazing. However, at other times he seemed to miss crucial elements of the scene. It was as if he perceived a location that was *almost* the place as it is on Earth, but not quite. Why should this be if he is simply describing what he was actually seeing? Did he miss things because they simply were not there?

Robert Monroe was similar. When he travelled in the place he called 'Locale 1', he consistently perceived things that were not fully correct. This, to me, is strange. Like Swann, how could he be partly right and partly wrong about a scene he 'saw' in his mind's eye? If he was simply deluding himself, he would have seen nothing accurately. Of course, he could model a scene from memory and populate that with guesswork, but that simply cannot explain how he knew that Dr Bradshaw was taking a walk with his wife when Robert had expected him to be in bed. It does not explain how he accurately described Charles Tart's new house in California and yet 'saw' people who were not there at the time. Oddly, he also claimed that he interacted and communicated with people in this hypnagogic state – Dr Bradshaw acknowledged his presence and the laboratory technician congratulated him on his success in getting out of his body. However, neither individual recalled any such communication. Again, this adds to my belief that Monroe was describing something that really happened to him. Why not state that Dr Bradshaw did recall speaking with a disembodied Monroe, or indeed just simply not mention his attempt at communication? Who would have contradicted this, years after the event? No, this is a man who comes across as being honest and describes events as he perceived them.

For me the clue lies in Monroe's own cosmology. He suggests that there are three 'Locales'. Locale 1 is this world, Locale 2 the equivalent of the world of dreams, and Locale 3 is somewhere else entirely. Could it be that in reality there are only two locales, 2 and 3? Locale 1 is, in effect, either a hypnagogic illusion or else another version of Locale 3 that is *nearly* identical to our normal reality. This would certainly explain the errors of perception that are regularly reported by OOB experiencers. Could it be that they are confusing 'here' with 'somewhere else'?

This is exactly the conclusion drawn by modern ecsomatic traveller William Buhlman. He wrote:

> Slowly I came to understand that the environment
> I was observing was not the physical world, as I had

assumed. I realized that the structures I normally observed when out-of-body were non-physical structures ... Now I finally understood why there were slight variations between the non-physical and physical furniture and other objects. For example, the non-physical walls were often a different color, and the shapes and styles of some of the furniture and rugs were different. Much of this was minor but nevertheless noticeable ... It appears that we are not observing the physical world from a different perspective, as many believe, but are interacting in a separate but parallel dimension of energy.[61]

Earlier I discussed how in recent years it has been discovered that the highly psychedelic substance DMT is not only internally generated within the body, but is also a potentially crucial neurotransmitter within the brain itself. According to psychologist Rick Strassman, this fascinating substance may be generated within the pineal gland and, at a certain crucial time, floods the surrounding brain tissue causing a fully altered state of consciousness of the person affected. As we have already discussed, his associate Beach Barrett has gone one step further and suggests that the pineal gland is, in effect, a wormhole that uses the principle of an Einstein-Rosen Bridge to project consciousness into a parallel reality.

Could this be the *somewhere else* that OOB experiencers go? Indeed, by applying Everett's Many-Worlds Interpretation and David Bohm's implicate order, I may even be able to explain why there are no persuasive cases of veridical perception during an ecsomatic experience. This is because the experiencer is no longer in this universe, but in another one very 'close by'.

False Awakenings

Taken to its logical conclusion, the Everett Many-Worlds Interpretation proposes that every outcome of every decision manifests itself in a huge, ever increasing macroverse, and this has been taking place since the first few seconds of the Big Bang. Indeed, some modern physicists use this model to argue against another cosmological theory called the Anthropic Cosmological Principle. This points out the amazing series of fortuitous coincidences occurring in the first few seconds of the Big Bang and ensuring that life would evolve somewhere in the universe. These coincidences continued across billions of years and, in doing so, fine-tuned conditions for the evolution of life on this planet that would eventually become conscious, self-conscious and ultimately, reflectively self-conscious. Some have even suggested that the universe had to create such awareness in order to bring itself into existence by the future-creating 'observers' to collapse the wave function. Why this argument is so beguiling for many, particularly religious believers, is that this was all achieved at the first attempt. In other words, if there is only one universe then it only had one chance, against all the odds, to 'get it right first time'. However, and this is the really clever bit, if Everett was right and there are trillions of universes, then life and consciousness would have the right set of circumstances in many of these universes and we happen to inhabit one of them.

What this means is that there are literally millions, possibly billions, of versions of you and I, and every human being that has ever existed. In fact it gets more complex. There will be many more semi-versions of all of us as well. Remember, if your parents had not made the decisions they did, then you may have been conceived at a different time by a different sperm. Would this be still you or a subtly different version of you carrying the same DNA? A different month would involve a different egg. Same DNA but will this be the same person? The complexity then fans out across all the choices that all your ancestors made. A choice of location to live, a decision to emigrate to another part of the world and many other such decisions change everything for all future generations within that universe.

Now I am going to make it really complex by pointing out that each version of you will 'create' a life from the Akashic Field that surrounds them. This life will then be 'encoded' within the 'Bohmian' enfoldment within you. So, deep within your brain is a holographic record of every life that you could possibly live. In my previous books I call this the *Bohmian IMAX*. When applied to ecsomatic experiences this can fully explain why it is that veridical evidence during a Locale 1 OOB or NDE is impossible.

I would like to call these inwardly generated experiences 'intra-somatic'. The word 'ecsomatic' means 'outside the body', whereas my new term suggests an experience coming from deep within the body. This does not suggest that, because it is inwardly generated it is not 'real' – far from it. These experiences are probably more real than any phenomenal world experiences.

In this model, when someone has the sensation of leaving their body, they are actually moving into inner, not outer, space. The tingling sensation reported by many experiencers is brought about by the flowing of DMT (metatonin) through the synapses of the brain. Consciousness is then pulled inwards to the deepest areas in the brain and enters an Einstein-Rosen Bridge that allows immediate access to the information contained within the zero-point field (Akashic Field). It will be recalled that, according to Professor Ervin Laszlo, the quantum vacuum – a state that should contain absolutely nothing – has been found to be full of a new and seemingly limitless form of energy. It is seriously suggested that this zero-point energy contains vast amounts of information. If David Bohm is correct and what we perceive as reality is a holographically generated illusion, then each location point within that hologram can be accessed within the field. So, when the person enters the ZPF they may find themselves located anywhere as a point of consciousness.

It may be that in the borderline state they are perceiving a slightly different Everett universe in which everything may seem exactly as it is in their home location. The only difference is that they are viewing it from a seemingly impossible position, such as near the ceiling. They will look down and see another version of themselves lying in bed. In this part of the ZPF they are not trapped in a body, as they are in their usual Locale, and they can 'travel' within this facsimile and perceive information and interact with others. But this information is not the same as in Locale 1. There will be subtle differences. This is literally a 'mind generated' illusion that has its own external reality, if that makes sense.

On returning through the wormhole and back to Locale 1, the person wakes up and reports the oddest dream. This dream feels so real that they are convinced they were actually outside their body moving in external consensual space. However, the things they recall do not quite match the reality of Locale 1. They may describe speaking to people who, on subsequent questioning, do not confirm such a conversation; remember Robert Monroe's encounter with Dr Bradshaw and his subsequent interactions with the female technicians in Dr Tart's laboratory. They may try to read documents or record numbers, but they simply do not see them. This is because they are looking in the wrong place!

Another regularly reported phenomenon is 'false awakenings'. This is when the subject wakes up and gets up out of bed, usually in the dead of night when the person wishes to visit the toilet. They get up, walk across the room and turn round to see themselves lying in bed. They then wake up again and do the same thing, only to discover they are encountering a dream within a dream. I believe these dreams are exactly that – dreams. The person moves within a seemingly three-dimensional 'reality' that is very well known to them. It is fair to assume that the dream just creates a subjective model of the external location and places the dreamer within this creation.

A similar experience is termed 'sleep paralysis'. As we have seen, this disturbing sensation is generated by a neurological state known as REM Intrusion. This is where the person wakes up and feels paralysed. It is extremely disturbing and is usually accompanied by the feeling that there is malevolent entity present – a cowelled figure in the corner of the room or a gnome-like being sitting on the chest and adding to the sensation of being pinned down. You will recall that this is exactly the sensation produced when Olaf Blanke stimulated the left angular gyrus of his patients and when Michael Persinger had his 'God Helmet' stimulate the temporal lobes of his volunteers.

The suggested explanation for sleep paralysis is that metatonin's sister neurotransmitter, melatonin is responsible. As we have already seen, this substance is activated during times of darkness and it facilitates sleep by effectively paralysing the body. This allows the body to disassociate from the brain and stop any potential damage occurring if the sleeping body is moved around by the sleeping mind. Usually this is activated soon after the mind is deeply asleep. However, sometimes a burst of metatonin brings the mind to a quasi-awareness in which it is both accessing information from the zero-point field and is semi-awake. There is a very real sense of paralysis together with the encountering of a presence brought up from the deep subconscious. Indeed, in acknowledgement of the Monroe model, this could be a manifestation from Locale 2.

The Zero Point Field

Much earlier in our quest to understand the out-of-body experience I cryptically mentioned a potential new form of energy that may forever solve the world crisis of the inevitable depletion of our carbon-based energy reserves. Called zero-point energy, or ZPE, this resource can be found literally everywhere and offers such potential that already patents have been awarded to devices designed to process and convert it into a usable resource.

What has been missed by many commentators, however, is that ZPE also has profound implications for our understanding of exactly what makes the universe work and, in turn, this energy source may hold the key to the greatest mystery of all – consciousness.

So what do we mean when we use the term zero-point energy? Well, to begin understanding this new concept we have to disregard most of what we have been taught about the nature of a vacuum.

Most people given a basic education in the sciences are taught that space is exactly that – empty. Of course, on Earth no space is ever *really* empty, but outer space is a different concept altogether. By definition it is empty of anything. In the 19th century the idea that outer space was really empty was a huge issue. The problem was a simple one – electromagnetic energy. As we have already discussed, it was a known scientific 'fact' that light was a wave and that it travelled through space as a sound wave travelled though air. Therein lay the problem. Sound, in itself, does not exist. It is simply a compression wave in the air, travelling like waves travel in the water (which again, if you think about it, would not exist if there was no water – no water to wave, no wave!). But it was clear that light waves did travel through the vacuum of outer space. So how did light and heat get from the Sun to the Earth? What was doing the 'waving'?

In an attempt to solve this enigma, Victorian scientists proposed that space was not empty but contained a substance that carried the electromagnetic waves through space. This substance was called the 'luminiferous aether'. Its role was made clear by the word 'luminiferous' which means 'light carrying'. However, there was no evidence that this invisible substance existed except as a tool for one scientific paradigm to remain unchallenged against all the counter-evidence. In 1887, two American researchers, Albert Michelson and Edward Morley, proved, in a very ingenious experiment, that the luminiferous aether did not exist.

This was one of the first discoveries that contributed to the concept of the present paradigm of science. If light was a wave – which experimentation clearly proved it was – then how could it travel through empty space?

Remember that in 1905 Albert Einstein proved that light was also particulate – it was made up of tiny individual particles called photons. The problem of light propagation was solved. Particles exist in their own right and therefore do not need a medium in which to travel. Therefore, light particles could easily fly through space from the Sun to the Earth.

It is ironic that recent discoveries regarding the nature of space itself may suggest that we are in need of another paradigm change. In a curious echo from the past, it seems that a substance similar to the aether may indeed fill up all of space. This is known as the zero-point field – a field that fills all of space and is, in many ways, the backdrop to what we call 'reality'.

As discussed earlier, a 'field' is a medium by which information is transferred from one particle to another. We saw how the electromagnetic field exists everywhere. Well, that is not quite true; at absolute zero all known forms of energy, including electromagnetic energy, vanish. This really is 'empty space', and it is thought that this is where the zero-point field (ZPF) exists. Indeed, it is called 'zero-point' because it is found at the point of absolute zero temperature.

By international agreement, absolute zero is defined as 0K on the Kelvin scale, −273.15°C on the Celsius scale and −459.67°F on the Fahrenheit scale.

This is a very strange place, in many ways linked to the quantum world simply by its very environment. But what is of great significance to me in my search for an explanation of ecsomatic experiences, is that at these super-low temperatures another phenomenon takes place – the creation of the Bose-Einstein condensates. Could it be that within the deepest inner space of the smallest possible size and at the lowest possible temperature, the very place that David Bohm suggested that his 'implicate order' would be located, zero-point energy provides the fuel to create the Bose-Einstein condensates? Could this be the unified model that we have been looking for? According to world-renowned Hungarian philosopher Ervin Laszlo, the zero-point field is the ultimate ground state of the universe. Indeed, in his book *Science and the Akashic Field* he goes further and suggests that the ZPF is the ground state of *everything* – the Akasha of the great Eastern religions and philosophies, the place that contains the records of every single thing that has taken place within the universe, and possibly every single thing that will take place until the Big Crunch, and maybe even afterwards.

Suddenly, there is no such thing as empty space or a genuine vacuum, even at absolute zero. Zero-point energy (ZPE) is the ZPF equivalent of electromagnetic energy and is therefore even more ubiquitous than photons. It is literally everywhere. This includes the empty space within the atom. It may come as a surprise to you, but approximately 99.99 per cent of your body is made up of what used to be thought of as empty space. Every element in your body is made up of trillions of molecules. In turn, each molecule consists of atoms in a particular configuration. Most people assume that atoms are little hard billiard balls. They are not. As we have already discovered, they are mostly, if not entirely made up of empty space, consisting of a tiny nucleus with electrons spinning round in a cloud of probabilities. Again, these forms are nearly all made up of empty space. Now this is real space because, unlike outer space, objects can exist there, but in atomic and nuclear space there literally is nothing but ZPE.

Now here is the real mind-blowing point. Professor Laszlo believes that the Akashic Record of the mystics and the Theosophists is identical to the zero-point field. He calls this new concept the 'Akashic Field'. If we add to this the role of microtubules, as the intermediaries between the quantum world and that of the world that we perceive, then we are developing a challenging model of consciousness.

It is logical to conclude that the microtubules of the brain could have a direct communication with the ZPF and, by implication, Laszlo's Akashic Field, through the form of electromagnetic energy I discussed earlier, the enigmatic 'coherent light'.

This is significant, since it has been suggested by Japanese physicists Isuki Hirano and Atsushi Hirai that each micropulse of light generates single-photon holograms. Now, there are literally trillions of microtubules in the human body. If each one can create single-photon holograms then the amount of information that the human body can store is effectively unlimited.[62]

In another research paper, Peter Marcer and Walter Schempp have shown that microtubule communication across the body works in a non-local fashion. In other words, information is sent instantaneously between different locations within the body.[63]

But the single most amazing fact about microtubules is that any two closely situated parallel microtubules will give off an intense beam of light of a single wavelength in the direction of its partner. Encoded within these bands could be huge amounts of information.

This coherent light is generated from Bose-Einstein condensates deep within the brain itself. As we have seen, this peculiar state of matter functions in a state of non-local communication. Even more significant, however, is that B-E condensates come into existence when a dilute gas is cooled to a state just above absolute zero. In effect this means that B-E condensates must acquire their energy from a source other than the electromagnetic spectrum. Is it reasonable to suggest that this energy source may be the ZPF and, by implication the Akashic Field?

If this is the case then it is the process by which consciousness can acquire limitless information. The encoded data from the ZPF is uploaded by the B-E condensates in the form of coherent light. This coherent light then generates single-photon holograms between closely located microtubules. These generate interference patterns that can then be communicated across the brain in a non-local way.

Is this how remote viewing may work? Is the distance viewer literally drawing up enfolded information from the depths of the ZPF? This would certainly explain why it is that the information is unpredictable and dream-like. Indeed, there is a reasoned argument to suggest that sometimes the location that is experienced may be on an Earth but not this one. If we apply Everett's Many-Worlds scenario to our model then sometimes the distance viewer may perceive the same location on another version of Earth.

From this one can also explain how Monroe's Locale 2 and Locale 3 are to be found in alternative universes. Here is also a possibility that even Locale 1, which may seem very like 'reality' is, in fact, a closely related but not identical Earth located in another Everett universe. The details of this Earth can be uploaded from the ZPF and presented to consciousness as a three-dimensional holographic image that will seem, and in fact probably is in some way, real.

In an earlier chapter I discussed how Tom Campbell and his associate Dennis Mennerich designed the HemiSync® process by placing the brain in a state of what is known as 'synchrony'. This state seems to open up consciousness in such a way that it accesses the Akashic Field directly. In this way people who use the HemiSync claim that they travel out of their body and to other places; clearly the same as Robert Monroe's Locales 2 and 3. But there is more to this. It seems that the production of synchronized, coherent electromagnetic energy in the brain at a given frequency leads to 'laser-like' conditions. This in turn brings about a synchrony between the two hemispheres of the brain.

In my second book, *The Daemon – A Guide To Your Extraordinary Secret Self,* I suggest that all human beings consist of two independent consciousnesses. I call these the *Daemon* and the *Eidolon.* The Eidolon is located in the dominant hemisphere of the brain and is the 'everyday' self, the being that calls itself 'I' or 'me'. The inhabitant of the non-dominant hemisphere, the Daemon, is a much more complex entity. Indeed, this being has access to considerable amounts of information denied to the Eidolon. In simple terms this is the 'Higher Self', the 'Overself' or the *Neshamah* of the Kabbalah. I further suggest that there can be a situation in which the Daemon and the Eidolon can become a single, unitary being. I call this being the 'Dyad' and I suggest that this is the state that many adepts and spiritually advanced human beings achieve after many 'incarnations'. Moreover, it is highly possible that the application of any process that brings about synchrony in the brain can short-cut this evolution, albeit for a very short amount of time.

However beguiling this model may seem, it does have its problems. The major issue is that B-E condensates can only exist at extremely low temperatures. The human brain is a very warm, wet place where the ambient temperature is 98.6 degrees Fahrenheit, whereas B-E condensates have only been demonstrated at –459 degrees Fahrenheit. This has been picked up by particle physicist Max Tegmark, who points out that the wave function may exist in a coherent state, but only for a tiny amount of time before rapidly decohering within the warm, wet environment of the brain. He calculated this as being somewhere in the region of 100 'femtoseconds'.[64]

But the single-photon holograms suggested by Hirano and Hirai need exactly the warm temperatures found within the cellular fluids that immerse the microtubules.

In my first book *Is There Life After Death? – The Extraordinary Science of What Happens When We Die*, I suggest that the human mind records every event, thought and feeling experienced during a lifetime. Furthermore I suggest that this 'recording' is played back at the moment of death in what is known as the 'Panoramic Life Review' by researchers into the near-death experience (NDE). I call this recording the *Bohmian IMAX* in honour of David Bohm. After researching material for this book, I have concluded that the 'BIMAX' is more than simply a brain-generated memory, it is, in reality, the dying person accessing their own section of the Akashic Field (ZPF) through the interaction of ZPE and B-E condensates within the microtubules. This is a broadening of the exclusively ZPF model of Laszlo, the B-E condensates of Hirano and Hirai and the microtubule wave-function collapse of Penrose and Hamerhoff. I would like to therefore expand my originally limited model of the internally generated 'panoramic' life review to encompass this much wider, and more satisfactory, model but still describe it as the Bohmian IMAX.

Could this be what is really happening when certain individuals find themselves in other locations? In my opinion, regular OOB experiences resulting in an experiencer viewing their own body from an external viewpoint, can be explained by applying the results of the experiments of Olaf Blanke and Henrik Ehrsson discussed in Chapter Eight. This may be an elaborate illusion and, as such, this would explain the paucity of veridical information in support of the idea that it is a 'real' experience. However, I believe that the 'travelling clairvoyance' and remote viewing are quite different phenomena, as are lucid dreaming and travels in other dimensions.

In my opinion, the ZPF model really does suggest an explanation of the ecsomatic experience that transcends the present stand-off between materialism and idealism. Neither position is right or wrong. It is the base-line understanding of the workings of the universe that is at fault.

For example, let us take the Kabbalist concepts of Hokmah, Kether and Yesod, and apply my interpretation of what these esoteric concepts signify within my revised model.

Hokmah incorporates all the wavelengths of light that can be perceived by the mind. As we have seen, it is possible that the visible part of the electromagnetic spectrum stimulates the production of DMT within the pineal gland. This, in turn, generates a perception of inner light when applied in a stroboscopic pattern, such as that generated by Winkler and Proeckl's LL-stimulator. According to Dubuis, Hokmah is also experienced by the ecsomatic mind as a realm of spacelessness, or, more specifically, a place where everything that is within Creation exists in the same place. Is this not exactly how Laszlo describes the zero-point field? Indeed, this also has huge echoes of David Bohm's implicate order.

Kether is defined as 'the Crown'. According to the Zohar this is the 'most hidden of all things'. Other esotericists, such as Dion Fortune, described Kether as a point that crystallizes out of the vastness of the unmanifest infinity known as the *Ein Sof*. A variation of this is the *Ain Sof Aur* which translates from Hebrew as 'endless light'. Such a point location that contains huge amounts of light could be interpreted as a black hole or, more accurately, the other end of an Einstein-Rosen bridge, an object known as a 'white hole', in which light emanates.

The astrophysicist Stephen Hawking has suggested that the zero-point field may be full of tiny black holes. Technically known as 'quantum mechanical black holes' these tiny objects may be only slightly larger than the smallest possible piece of space, the 'Planck length'. As we know this is the unbelievably tiny distance of 10^{-33} centimetres. If Hawking is correct then these tiny black holes will fill all empty space, in effect turning a vacuum into a plenum. Therefore the human brain has trillions upon trillions of these objects, all sucking in electromagnetic energy. Each one of these is a potential Einstein-Rosen bridge. What is even more intriguing is that, where there are micro black holes, there will also be micro white holes spewing out light. As this light will consist of photons that are 'entangled', it will be coherent and, as we already know, coherent light generated in this way is known as a Bose-Einstein condensate. These condensates flow out of the zero-point field and stimulate the trillions of microtubules within the billions of neurons to create the holographic experience we have come to know as 'reality'. If this is correct then the external world is internally generated, and is an intensely personal perception built up from our own psychological history and the experiences of every human being that has ever lived and ever will exist. This is the zero-point field, also known as the Akashic Record.

Have we a potential answer to the mystery of the ecsomatic experience? For centuries the word 'enlightenment' has been used to describe the opening up of consciousness to hidden truths and mystic experiences. Could it be that this is the ultimate discovery; that we are enlightened by light and that reality has many, many more levels then we can imagine?

Epilogue

My encounter with Lucia in Geneva was followed by a dinner party. Evelyn, Engelbert, Dirk, Engelbert's son Elias and I were joined by déjà-vu expert Dr Arthur Funkhouser, researcher Mike Horner and a Croatian-born Canadian by the name of Pier Rubesa. We discussed many areas of mutual interest and a wonderful evening was had by all. However, I was still in a curious state of mind; the events of the afternoon had brought about a profound change in me. I somehow felt more alive and my senses seemed more attuned to what was going on around me. Furthermore, something of significance happened later, after I had retired. I awoke in the early hours of the morning with a peculiar sensation in the centre of my forehead. It was like a small snake was moving around about three inches above the bridge of my nose. Whatever I did the sensation remained. Sometimes it felt like a vibration and at other times it felt more like a throbbing. It was not disturbing in any way, but it certainly was strange.

The next day I found myself being whisked along the shores of Lake Geneva to a small town called Clarens, just outside Montreux. Mike, Evelyn and I were on our way to Pier's Center of Bioharmonic Research on the shores of the lake. We arrived mid-morning, with the lake looking like a huge sheet of glass reflecting the French mountains on the opposite side. It was an idyllic spot.

Pier was keen for me to add to my 'Lucia' event by giving me the opportunity to experience another mind-altering scenario. In his studio he has rigged up three huge loudspeakers that are linked to his computer. He can modulate the frequencies of the sound in such a way that the sound waves can be focused on one spot. This is where the subject is located within the room.

For the second time in two days I found myself lying flat and concentrating on an outside source of sensory stimulation. This time it was sound. Just as with the LL-stimulator, it took a few minutes for my brain to attune to what was taking place. I suddenly sensed something that I recognized immediately. I felt a tingling in the veins in my arm. I could feel the blood running through them and then, as expected, I felt the blood start to vibrate and a feeling of tightness around my head. I have had this sensation many times in my life, but this was the first time for about five years or so. I recognized it as being something colloquially known as 'Chinese Restaurant Syndrome'. As soon as this started, I knew that it was of great significance.

The medical profession knows that CRS is caused by an 'allergic' reaction to the food additive monosodium glutamate. Clearly the ambient sounds coming at me from three different directions had modulated each other to a single, pure tone. This tone was stimulating the production of the neurotransmitter glutamate within the synapses of my brain. As we have already discovered, glutamate is the key chemical messenger in the temporal and frontal lobes, and is central to the function of the hippocampus. Dr Karl Jansen at the Maudsley Hospital in London has shown that this neurotransmitter may be responsible for near-death experience as well as facilitating temporal lobe epilepsy and migraine auras. What Pier's soundscape was creating in my brain was a classic 'altered state of consciousness', and what happened next, therefore, should have come as no surprise to me, but it did. The vibrating in my pineal gland started again, only this time it was much gentler than with the LL-stimulator. I then felt that I was rocking from side to side as if in a small boat on a choppy sea. After a few seconds this subsided and the soundscape ceased. My second 'trip' in two days had come to an end, and so had my old understanding of the word 'reality'.

According to the late philosopher-mathematician Michael Whiteman, our understanding of the ultimate workings of the universe cannot be complete because the ruling world-view is, as he termed it, 'one-level naturalism'.[65] He described this as:

> Firstly there is just one real space and time …
> secondly, the only 'realities' are point particles
> and fields … thirdly, there exists a complete set of
> mathematical laws by means of which the measures
> for particles and fields are exactly determined for
> all future time.[66]

One-level naturalism is no longer an adequate model by which we try to measure the observed nature of the universe. As we have already discovered, quantum physics shows that matter is built from a substance that has wave-like properties that are collapsed into point objects by the act of observation or measurement. Einstein showed that there is nothing absolute about space and time. Indeed, I fully agree with Whiteman that this model cannot even begin to explain consciousness, the self, free will, meaning, knowledge or morality. Whiteman made a wonderfully precise description of this error; he stated that we confuse 'reality with appearance'.[67]

This is the position I was at as I started my research for this book. However, as I discovered more about the ecsomatic phenomenon, I realized that I would never find 'proof' that such experiences happen in consensual reality because, by their very nature, these perceptions cannot be measured by any known scientific metric. Most writers and researchers, myself included, have tried to find answers using Whiteman's one-level naturalism. Even the experiencers themselves have understood their perceptions to be part of this model; this is why they consistently fail to prove their ecsomatic experiences when asked to supply veridical evidence of their out-of-body perceptions.

After my two experiences in Switzerland, I now know exactly why the ecsomatic state is such a wonderfully enlightening perception, and, once experienced, the world becomes a very different place.

My pineal gland is now active and I await the next development in this exciting first-person game called *Life*.

Notes

1 Segal, Suzanne, *Collision with the Infinite*, p49, Blue Dove Press, 1998

2 Kowalski, Marek; Rubin, David ,'Improved Cosmological Constraints from New, Old and Combined Supernova Datasets', *The Astrophysical Journal* 686, pp749–78, University of Chicago Press, 27 October 2008

3 Stavish, Mark, *Between The Gates – Lucid dreaming, Astral Projection and the Body of Light in Western Esotericism*, pp103–4, Weiser Books, 2008

4 Blavatsky, HP, *The Key To Theosophy*, p121, Theosophical University Press, 2002

5 Hinckley, Bryant S, *The Faith of Our Pioneer Fathers*, p183, Deseret,1959

6 Hinckley, Bryant S, *The Faith of Our Pioneer Fathers*, p183, Deseret,1959

7 Clark, Kimberley, 'Clinical interventions with near-death experiencers' in *The Near-death Experience; Problems, Prospects, Perspectives*, B Greyson & C P Flynn (eds), pp242–55, Charles C Thomas, 1984

8 van Lommel, P, *et al*, 'Near-death experience in Survivors of Cardiac Arrest: A Prospective Study in the Netherlands', *The Lancet* 358, pp2039–45, 2001

9 Smit, Rudolf H, 'Corroboration of the Denture Anecdote Involving Veridical Perception in a Near-death Experience', *Journal of Near-death Studies* V.27, No 1, 2008

10 Lindley, JH; Bryan, S & Conley, B, 'Near-death experiences in a Pacific Northwest population: *The Evergreen study* – *Anabiosis* 1. p109, 1981

11 Lindley, JH; Bryan, S & Conley, B, 'Near-death experiences in a Pacific Northwest population: *The Evergreen study* – *Anabiosis* 1, p110, 1981

12 Augustine, K, 'Hallucinatory Near-Death Experiences' Infidels Net (2008) and a shorter version, 'Near-Death experiences with Hallucinatory Features' – *Journal of Near-Death Studies* 26, 1, pp3–31, 2007

[13] Holden, Janice M, 'Visual Perception During Naturalistic Near-death Out-of-body Experiences', *Journal of Near-Death Studies* 7, pp107–20

[14] Holden, Janice M, 'Visual Perception During Naturalistic Near-death Out-of-body Experiences', *Journal of Near-Death Studies* 7, pp107–20

[15] Holden, Janice M & Joesten, Leroy, 'Near-death veridicality research in the hospital setting: Problems and Promise', *Journal of Near-Death Studies* 9,1, p46, 1990

[16] Greyson, B; Holden, JM & Mounsey, JP, 'Failure to Elicit Near-death Experiences in Induced Cardiac Arrest', *Journal of Near-Death Studies* 25, 2, pp85–98, 2006

[17] *Daily Telegraph*, 18 September 2008

[18] Ring, K & Elsaesser-Valarino, E, *Lessons from the Light*, p77, Moment Point Press, 2006

[19] Ring, K & Elsaesser-Valarino, E, *Lessons from the Light*, pp73–97, Moment Point Press, 2006

[20] Monroe, Robert A, *Journeys Out of the Body*, p30, Broadway Books, 2001

[21] Monroe, Robert A, *Journeys Out of the Body*, p47, Broadway Books, 2001

[22] Monroe, Robert A, *Journeys Out of the Body*, p71, Broadway Books, 2001

[23] Tart, Charles T, 'Six Studies of Out-of-the-Body Experiences', *Journal of Near-Death Studies*, March 1997

[24] Monroe, Robert A, *Journeys Out of the Body*, p87, Broadway Books, 2001

[25] Monroe, Robert A, *Journeys Out of the Body*, p131, Broadway Books, 2001

[26] Monroe, Robert A, *Journeys Out of the Body*, p24, Broadway Books, 2001

[27] Swann, Ingo, *To Kiss Earth Goodbye*, pp118–19, Dell, 1975

[28] Targ, Russell & Puthoff, Harold, *Mind Reach*, p26, Hampton Roads, 2005

[29] Targ, Russell & Puthoff, Harold, *Mind Reach*, pp27, 28, Hampton Roads, 2005

[30] Targ, Russell & Puthoff, Harold, *Mind Reach*, p2, Hampton Roads, 2005

[31] Targ, Russell & Puthoff, Harold, *Mind Reach*, p208, Hampton Roads, 2005

[32] Targ, Russell & Puthoff, Harold, *Mind Reach*, p210, Hampton Roads, 2005

[33] Vieira, Waldo, *Projections of the Consciousness – A Diary of Out-of-body Experiences*, p59, IAC, 2007

[34] Campbell, Thomas, *My Big Toe – Book 1, Awakening*, p76, Lightening Strike Books, 2007

[35] http://www.eckankar.org/soultravel.html

[36] Twemlow, Gabbard & Jones, 'The out-of-body experience: A Phenomenological Typology Based on Questionnaire Responses', *Am. J. Psychiatry* 139, pp450–5, April 1982

[37] Monroe, Robert, *Journeys Out of the Body*, p28, Broadway, 2001

[38] Waggoner, Robert, *Lucid Dreaming – Gateway to the Inner Self*, Moment Point Press, 2009

[39] Campbell, Thomas, *My Big Toe*, Lightening Strike Books, 2003

[40] Yuschek, Thomas, *Advanced Lucid Dreaming*, p9, Lulu, 2006

[41] Yuschek, Thomas, *Advanced Lucid Dreaming*, p164, Lulu, 2006

[42] Monroe, Robert, *Journeys Out of the Body*, p26, Broadway, 2001

[43] Twemlow, SW & Gabbard, G, *With the Eyes of the Mind: An Empirical Analysis of Out-of-the-Body States*, 1984

[44] Wilson, Ian, 'Interview with Robert Waggoner', *The Lucid Dream Exchange*, June 2010

[45] Blanke, O; Ortigue, S; Landis, T & Seeck, M, 'Stimulating own-body perceptions', *Nature* 419, pp269–70, 2002

[46] Olney *et al*, 'Excito-toxic mechanisms of epileptic brain damage', *Advances in Neurology* 44, pp857–77, 1986

[47] Jansen, KLR, 'Neuroscience and the near-death experience: roles for the NMDA-PCP receptor, the sigma receptor and endopsychosins', *Medical Hypotheses* 31, pp25–9, 1990

[48] Jansen, KLR, 'Neuroscience, Ketamine and the Near-Death Experience' in *The Near Death Experience*, L Bailey and J Yates eds, Routledge, 1996

[49] Grinspoon, L & Bakalar, S, *Psychedelic Drugs Reconsidered*, Basic Books, New York, 1981

[50] Quirion *et al*, 'Evidence for an endogenous peptide ligand for the phencyclidine receptor', *Peptides* 5, pp967–77, 1984

[51] Carr, DB, 'Endorphins at the approach of death', *Lancet* 1, p390, 1981

[52] Carr, DB, 'On the evolving neurobiology of the near-death experience' *Journal of Near Death Studies* 7, pp251–4, 1989

[53] Fontanilla *et al*, 'The Hallucinogen N,N-Dimethyltryptamine (DMT) Is an Endogenous Sigma-1 Receptor Regulator', *Science*, Vol 323, no 5916, pp934–7, Feb 2009

[54] http://metatoninresearch.org/Home.html

[55] Monroe, Robert A, *Journeys Out of the Body*, p24, Broadway Books, 1977

[56] Feynman, R, *The Character of Physical Law,* p29, Penguin, London, 1992

[57] I know of two excellent non-technical explanations of Bell's Inequality. One can be found on pages 227–31 of Dean Radin's book *Entangled Minds.* The other, slightly more technical, can be found on pages 143–51 of *Quantum Enigma – Physics Encounters Consciousness* by Bruce Rosenblum and Fred Kuttner.

[58] Aspect, A; Dalibaed, J & Roger, G, 'Experimental test of Bell's inequalities using time-varying analyzers', *Physical Review Letters* 49, p1804, 1982

[59] Marcikic, I; de Riedmatten, H; Tittel, W; Zbinden, H; Legre, M & Gisin, N, 'Distribution of time-bin entangled quibits over 50km of optical fibre', *Physical Review Letters* 93, 2004

[60] Bohm, D, *Wholeness and the Implicate Order*, p172, Routledge & Kegan Paul, 1980

[61] Buhlman, William, *Adventures Beyond the Body*, pp16–18, Harper, 1996

[62] Hirano, I & Hirai, N, 'Holography in the single photon region', *Applied Optics* 25, 1741–2, 1986

[63] Marcer, PJ & Schempp, W, 'Model of the neuron working by quantum holography', *Informatica* 21, pp514–19, 1997

[64] That is one quadrillionth, or one millionth of one billionth of a second. To appreciate just how short a period of time this is, a femtosecond is to a second, what a second is to about 31.7 million years.

[65] Whiteman, JHM, 'Quantum Theory & Parapsychology', *Journal of the American Society for Psychical Research* 67, pp341–61, 1973

[66] Whiteman, JHM, 'A three-tier ontology for parapsychology and modern physics', in *Parapsychology in South Africa*, JC Poynton (ed), p124, 1975

[67] Whiteman, JHM, *Old and New Evidence on the Meaning of Life Vol.1 – An Introduction to Scientific Mysticism*, Colin Smythe, 1986

Index

Akashic Field *see* zero-point field
Akashic Record, 25–6, 105
alpha-endopsychin, 143
altered states of consciousness
    (ASCs), 10, 26, 95, 101, 137, 173,
    191
    author's experience, xiv–xi, 210–11
    in Kabbalah, 21
    and Monroe's Locales, 139
    natural, brain-generated, 148–9
    perceptive differences, 120
    pineal gland gateway, 17, 194
    and sensory deprivation, 91–2
    shamanic, 12, 13
    and synchrony, 97–8
    in temporal lobe epilepsy, 69, 149
American Society for Psychical
    Research, 73
amines, 144
anaesthetics, 188–9
angular gyrus, 132–6, 198
anima mundi, 26
Anthropic Cosmological Principle,
    195
aquarium analogy, 176–7
archetypes, 13, 14, 15, 20, 64, 101
Aserinsky, Eugene, 130
Aspect experiment, 171, 172, 174,
    175, 176, 177, 187
Assiah, 20, 21
astral plane(s), 11, 20, 25, 65, 105, 106
atoms, 155–7, 201–2
Atziluth, 20
Augustine, Keith, 41
auras, migraine and epilepsy, 70
avatars, 115
AWARE Study, 47–8
Axelrod, Julius, 144
ayahuasca, 146

Backster, Clive, 73, 74
'bardo' state, 18
Barrett, Beach, 150–1, 194
baryonic matter, 7
beings and entities, 3, 15, 24, 57,
    64–5, 93, 101–2, 114, 137, 138,
    141, 147–8, 198
'Beings of Light', 30, 32, 33, 49, 50
Bell's Inequality, 171, 172, 187
Beriah, 20
Beyond the Mind-Body Problem
    symposium, 46–7
Big Bang, 173–4, 182, 183, 195
Big Computer, The (TBC), 102, 116
bi-location, 38, 63, 68–9, 71, 77
binaural beats, 97
black holes, 152
    in the brain, 207
blackbody radiation, 161
Blanke, Olaf, 133–4, 135, 136, 198,
    205–6
Blavatsky, Helena, 24, 96, 146–7
Bohm, David, 115, 173, 174–80, 184,
    194, 196–7, 201, 205, 206
Bohmian IMAX model, 9–10, 196,
    205
Bohr, Niels, 164, 170
Bön, 17, 18, 96
Born, Max, 164–5, 166
Bose-Einsteinian (B-E) condensates,
    186–7, 188, 201, 202–3, 204, 207
Bradshaw, Dr, 57–8, 60–1, 94, 185,
    193, 197
Brahman, 16, 17
brain
    black and white holes in, 207
    and consciousness, 4, 41, 91, 154,
    179–80
    Einstein-Rosen Bridges in, 196, 207
    empty space in, 152, 157, 175

generating altered states, 148–9
memory banks, 13–14, 132
microtubules in, 187, 202
and REM sleep, 131
synchrony state, 97–8, 203–4
unconsciousness, 112
warm, wet environment, 204–5
see also neurotransmitters; pineal
gland
brain cells, 139
brain waves, 95
alpha generation, 98
change through LL-stimulator,
xiii–xiv
Brennan, Herbie, 136
Bruce, Robert, 125
Buddha, 17, 24
Buddhism, 17–19, 23, 149
Buhlman, William, 193–4
Butler, Billy, 3, 5

Campbell, Tom, 68, 95, 96–7, 98, 106,
114, 115–16, 125, 147, 203–4
Big Toe (Theory of Everything)
model, 99–103, 115–16, 166
Carrington, Hereward, 96–7, 147
Centre for Continuous Consciousness
(CCC), 90
cerebral cortex, 133, 141
chakras, 24, 96
Cheatham, Sebastian, 13, 101
Cheating the Ferryman (CTF)
hypothesis, 121
Clark, Kimberley, 36–7
clear light of death, 18–19
clear light of sleep, 19
coherent light, 186, 188, 202–3, 207
collective unconscious, 102
Conscientiology, 90–1
consciousness
access to limitless information, 203
and anaesthetics, 188, 189
bi-location, 68, 71
Bön conception, 18
and the brain, 4, 41, 91, 154, 179–80
disappearance through a wormhole,

152, 194, 196
disembodied, 4–5, 9, 46, 47–8, 49, 91
enfolding of wholeness, 177, 190
evolution through reincarnation, 91
facilitation, 186
and foetal development, 149
microtubules key to, 187, 189
scientific understanding, 7
and zero-point field, 199, 202, 203
consensual hallucination, 86
consensual reality, xvi, 10–11, 93, 102,
110–11
Copenhagen Interpretation, 102, 162,
169, 170, 171, 174, 181
cultural norms, 100, 101

Daemon, The (Peake), 2, 204
Dalton, John, 155–6
dark energy, 7, 174
dark matter, 7, 174
de Broglie, Louis, 163–4
death, 16, 21, 91 *see also* clear light of
death; near-death experiences
Demmont, Bill, 130
Democritus, 155
'dentures' case, 37–9, 41
Descartes, René 96
DeWitt, Bryce, 182
Dick, Philip K, 67
dimethyltryptamine (DMT), 144–5,
146–9, 194, 196, 206
Dream Yoga, xiv, 18, 24
dreams and dreaming, 11, 21, 41, 42,
64, 101, 107, 138, 197, 198
precognitive, 121–5
vs. projections, 92–3
see also lucid dreaming
Dubuis, Jean, 21–3, 206
Dunne, J W, 122
dying while living, 104
Dzogchen teachings, 19, 24

Eckankar, 103–8
'ecsoma', 110
Ehrsson, Henrik, 134–5, 205–6
eidetic ('photographic') memory, 81

Einstein, Albert, 155, 159, 163, 164, 167, 168–70, 171, 174, 200, 211
Einstein-Rosen Bridge, 151–2, 194, 196
electromagnetic energy, 98, 199–200, 202, 204, 207
electromagnetic field, 76, 137, 159–60, 200
electromagnetic spectrum, 160–1, 206
electrons, 162–3, 164, 172, 174–5, 176, 202
elements, 156
Elsaesser-Valarino, Evelyn, xiii, 50, 209
empty space, 152–3, 157, 175, 199–200, 200–1, 207
endorphins, 140, 143
enlightenment, 17, 19, 96, 207
entanglement, 168–9, 171–2, 173–4, 185, 207
epilepsy, temporal lobe, 66, 69–70, 132, 141, 149, 210
EPR Paradox, 168–70
etheric body, 24–5, 110
Everett III, Hugh, 173, 180, 181–5, 195
Evergreen Study, 39, 40

false awakening, 110–12, 197–8
Faraday, Michael, 159
Fenwick, Peter, 44–5, 46, 47
Feynman, Richard, 165, 172, 183
Funkhouser, Arthur, 123, 209

Gabbard, Glen, 119–20
gamma rays, 160
Gautama Siddhartha, 17
Gell-Mann, Murray, 183
geographical coordinates, 78–84
glial cells, 139
glutamate, 140, 141, 210
glutamate flood, 142–3
Gnosticism, 19, 108
'God Helmet', 137, 198
Gross, Darwin, 104

Hamerhoff, Stuart, 186, 188

Hawking, Stephen, 183, 184–5, 207
Hebbard, Arthur, 75, 76
Heisenberg, Werner, 164–5
helium, 156
Helpers, 65, 66–7
HemiSync, 67, 95–9, 147, 203–4
Hermetic traditions, 23
Hertog, Thomas, 184–5
'hidden variables', 168, 174–6
Hinckley, Bryant S, 33
Hinduism, 16–17, 23
hippocampus, 141, 210
Hirai, Atsushi, 202, 205
Hirano, Isuku, 202, 205
Hokmah, 21, 22, 206
Holden, Janice, 42–3, 45–6
holograms, 178
holomovement, 115, 178
Hopi language, 100
hypnagogic state and imagery, 119, 120, 128–30, 131–2, 192, 193
hynopompic state and imagery, 120, 130, 131–2, 192

Immobilitarium, 91, 92, 132
implicate order, 162, 173, 174–80, 189–90, 194
International Academy of Consciousness (IAC), 90–5, 132
International Association of Near Death Studies (IANDS), 27, 41
2004 conference, 44, 46
introsomatic (inner) experience, 9–10, 11, 15, 88, 107, 108, 113, 179–80, 191–207
Io, 87, 180
Is There Life After Death? (Peake), 2, 205
Issels, Josef, 34–5

Jansen, Karl, 141, 142, 210
Janssen, Pierre, 156
Jesus, 24, 30, 50, 101
Joesten, Leroy, 42–3
Jupiter, remote viewing, 84–7, 172

Kabbala, 20–3, 206–7
Kerguelen, 81–2
ketamine, 141–3
Kether, 21, 22, 206
Kleitman, Nathaniel, 130–1
Klemp, Harold, 104
Kuhn, Thomas, 158

Large Hadron Collider, 179
Laszlo, Ervin, 196, 201, 202
Lawrence, Madelaine, 43–4
Leadbeater, C W, 25
Lenard, Philip, 163
life reviews, 32, 50, 205
light, 160, 206–7
    wave/particle duality, 163–4
    see also coherent light;
      photons
Linga Śarīra, 16–17
liquid crystals, 187
LL-stimulator (Lucia), xii–xvi, 18,
    206, 209
Locales, 57, 64–5, 95, 138–9, 193
    1, 57–65, 93, 138, 180, 185, 192–3,
      197, 203
    2, 64, 65, 93, 98, 138, 193, 198, 203
    3, 64, 65–8, 88, 93, 98, 138, 152, 173,
      185, 193, 203
lower world, shamanic, 12, 15, 101
lucid dreams and dreaming, 16, 18–19,
    21, 23, 56, 65, 107, 108, 112–26,
    148, 167, 206
    dream-induced (DILDS), 117, 119
    and the out-of-body state, 119–26
    wake-induced (WILDS), 117–18,
      119

magnetometer experiment, 75–6
Malaya experience, 3–5, 136
Mani, 108
Many Worlds (MWI), 162, 167, 173,
    182–4, 194, 195–6, 197, 203
Marcer, Peter, 202
'Maria's shoe' case, 35–7
Marshall, John, 28
Maxwell, James Clerk, 159

maya, 16
meditation, xiv, 150
melatonin, 149, 198
memories, 13–14, 100, 102, 118,
    132, 141, 142, 179 see also eidetic
    memory
Mennerich, Dennis, 95, 96–7, 98, 147,
    203–4
mental illness, 151
Mercury, remote viewing, 87
Merkawah Foundation, 38, 39
metatonin, 149–51, 198
Michelson, Albert, 200
microtubules, 187–8, 189, 202, 205,
    207
middle world (shamanistic), 13–14
migraine, 69, 70, 149, 210
Milbourne, Christopher, 73
mind
    and body, 48, 109
    creation of ecsomatic worlds, 9–10,
      13–14, 15, 18, 91–2, 102, 108, 117,
      166, 130, 197
    creation of reality, 19, 115, 125, 166,
      189–90
    and matter, 7, 158, 170, 182, 189
    three states, 18
Mitchell, Janet, 73, 79
molecules, 20, 157
monoamine oxidase (MAO), 150, 151
monosodium glutamate, 210
Monroe, Robert, 21, 52–70, 71, 88, 93,
    94, 95, 97–8, 111–12, 115, 118–19,
    138, 150–1, 152, 172, 173, 180,
    191–2, 192–3, 185, 197
Moody, Raymond, 28, 30–2
Morley, Edward, 200
Mormons, 33–4
Muldoon, Sylvan, 96–7, 147
multidimensional reality, 90

near-death experiences (NDEs), 23,
    26, 27–51, 101, 106, 112, 115, 141,
    142–3, 148, 205, 210
    blind individuals, 48–50
    evidence, 34–41

experiments, 41–8
Gallup survey, 32, 33
Moody's nine traits, 31–2, 49
neurology, 102, 128–37
neurons, 139, 140, 187
neurotransmitters, 139–41
Newton, Isaac, 158–9, 162
n-methyl-aspartate (NMDA)
    receptors, 142–3
non-locality, 69, 167–73, 187, 202, 203
non-physical matter reality (NPMR),
    98, 99, 101, 114, 116, 125, 166

'observer created universe', 184–5
ORCH-OR (Orchestrated Objective
    Reduction), 186–90
Orsted, Hans Christian, 159
Oster, Gerald, 97
Otis, Karl, 73–4

Pan's Labyrinth (del Toro film), 14
Parnia, Sam, 47
PCP receptors, 143
Penrose, Roger, 186, 189
peptides, 143
Persinger, Michael, 136–7, 198
photoelectric effect, 162–3
photons, 163, 164, 174, 186, 187, 200,
    202
  entanglement, 171, 207
  see also single-photon micropulses;
    single-photon holograms
physical matter reality (PMR), 99–101,
    102, 114, 116, 125
pineal gland, 17, 18, 25, 95–7, 104,
    106, 146–7, 149, 150, 194, 206,
    211, 212
  as wormhole, 151–2, 194
Planck, Max, 161
planes of existence
  Eckanar, 105–6
  Kabbalah, 21–3, 206–7
  Theosophy, 24
  Surat Shabd Yoga, 105
Plunkett, Gary, 13, 101
Podolsky, Boris, 168

portals, 14, 149, 151
precognition, 32, 121–5
probability waves, 164–5 see also wave
    function
Proeckl, Dirk, xiii–xiv, xv, 206, 209
Project Scanate, 81–4
Projectarium, 91–2, 132
Projectiology, 90, 91
protons, 75, 164, 168
psyche, Kabbalistic elements, 20–1
psychedelic drugs, 138–52
'psychosoma', 90–1
Puthoff, Harold, 74–84

quanta, 161, 162
quantum biology, 74, 75
quantum coherence, 186
quantum physics, 76, 154–90, 211
quantum potential, 175–6
quantum vacuum, 152–3, 175, 196
quarks, 75

'Rainbow Beings' 19
rebirth, 18–19
receptors, 140
reincarnation, 91
REM Intrusion, 119–20, 131–2, 198
REM sleep, 119, 130–1
remote viewing, 71–87, 98, 112, 148,
    167, 203, 206
Ring, Kenneth, 49, 50
Ritchie, George, 28–30, 95
Rogo, Scott, 76
roll-out technique, 59, 60, 65, 118
Rosen, Nathan, 168
Ruach (everyday self), 20–1
Rubesa, Pier, 209–10
Ruoho, Arnold, 144–5

Sabom, Michael, 32–3
Sant Mat, 104
Sapir, Edward, 100
Satori, Penny, 44, 46, 48
Schempp, Walter, 202
Schrödinger's cat, 180–1
science, need for new paradigm 7

Scientology, 103–4
Second Life, 102, 114–15, 116
Segal, Suzanne, 5–6, 7, 115, 119
sensory deprivation, 91–2, 132
sephiroth, 21–3
shabd (sound current), 104–5
shamanic drumming, 13
shamanic guides, 14
shamanism, 12–15, 17, 101–2
Sherman, Harold, 84, 85–6, 87, 88
siddhis, 17
sigma-1 receptors, 145, 148
single-photon holograms, 202, 203, 205
single-photon micropulses, 188
sleep paralysis, 41, 131, 150, 198
Smit, Rudolf H, 38
soul, 12, 18–19, 25, 96, 104, 149
soul travelling, 103, 105–8
spirit, 20, 24
Strassman, Richard, 146, 147–8, 194
subconscious, 15, 64, 93, 101, 130
subtle body (*Sukshma sharira*), 16–17
Sudar Singh, 103
superposition, 169, 184–5
Surat Shabd Yoga, 104, 107
Swann, Ingo, 21, 71–87, 95, 172, 180, 192
synapses, 140
synchrony, 98, 204
Szara, Stephen, 146

Targ, Russell, 77–84
Tart, Charles, 59–63, 68
Tarzs, Rebazar, 103
Tegmark, Max, 205
temporal-parietal junction (TPJ), right, 133
Theory of Everything (TOE) *see* Campbell, Tom
Theosophy, 23–6, 96
'third eye', 96, 106
Tibet, xiv, 17–18, 24
trace amine-associated receptors (TAARS), 144, 148
transcendence, 10–11

Tungus people, Siberia, 12
Twemlow, Stewart, 109, 111, 112, 119–20
Twitchell, Paul, 103–4

Umipeg, Vicki, 49–50
upper world, shamanic, 14–15, 101

van Lommel, Pim, 41–2
veridical evidence
    blind NDEs, 49–50
    examples, 35–40, 57–8
    experiments and tests, 42–8, 59–65
    lack of convincing, 68, 94–5, 121, 191, 192, 194, 196, 206, 212
vibrations, xv, xvi, 53–4, 56, 67, 95, 117, 150–1, 210, 211
Vieira, Waldo, 90, 92, 93–5
Von Neumann Proof, 174–5

Waggoner, Robert, 114, 124, 125, 167
wave function
    observation, and collapse of, 164, 165–6, 167–8, 169, 173, 180–1, 185, 189–90, 195, 211
    split into two realties, 182
wave/particle duality, 155, 163–4
white holes, 152, 207
Whiteman, Michael, 211
Whorf, Benjamin Lee, 100
Wilson, Ian, 121, 123–5, 167
Winkler, Engelbert, xiii–xiv, xv, xvi, 18, 206

Yechidah (Divine Self), 20–1
Yesod, 21, 22, 206
Yetzirah, 20, 21
YHVA, 20
Yost, Bill, 95
Young, Thomas, 163
Yuschak, Thomas, 116–18

zero-point energy (ZPE), 152–3, 196, 199, 201, 205
zero-point (Akashic) field (ZPF), 196, 200–7